I0832751

Memories from a Dusty Road

Memories from a Dusty Road

My Journey to the 21st Century

By Jerry McNeil

Published by
Hipnee Publications
Seattle, WA

Contact: j.t.mcneil@mac.com

All photographs are in the author's collection.

Cover photograph: Ben Siljestrom, 1951

ISBN 979-8-9938771-1-2

Library of Congress Card Number: 2025924779

Printed in the United States of America

Dedication

To my mother and father, who gave me unconditional love and support and guided me by example.

Preface

From a small gray house on a dusty gravel road to shaking hands with the President in the White House Rose Garden, this story shares my journey, highlighting my academic successes, setbacks, and struggles. My career goal was to become a high school teacher and coach in Colorado, but that didn't happen. I overcame many challenges through determination, a supportive home environment, and a bit of luck. I paved the way for a life filled with love, work, adventure, and fulfillment.

These pages are for my children and grandchildren. As they become interested, they will gain insight into my early life and understand the journey I took to reach this point. I plan to finish this book soon, so they have time to ask any questions they might have. They have heard stories before, but in my experience, it's often hard to remember what a parent or grandparent told you many years ago. Now, this will be something they can keep for decades.

This book isn't a biography or memoir; it's a collection of experiences. I included descriptions of my roles with the State of Colorado and the National Association of Counties, along with examples of key accomplishments and a mix of humorous and serious elements.

In my late 30s and 40s, I rediscovered my passion for baseball, meeting childhood heroes and legends from its golden era. Throughout my 50s, 60s, and 70s, I experienced incredible outdoor adventures, hiking and climbing across four continents.

I owe a great deal to Trish's encouragement and support for this project; without her involvement, I might have continued sharing stories that family and friends would likely forget. Now, this collection of my memories is available for family members who may someday be curious about my life. Her reviews, edits, and encouragement helped me stay focused. Without her, I wouldn't have been able to finish this book.

Table of Contents

Chapter 1: A Simple Life

My earliest memory is of going with my mother to Rondout Grammar School in 1951, where she worked as the school's cook. The old brick building opened as a one-room school in November 1917. By 1951, it had two classrooms, a kitchen, a dining room, and a rumpus room. The "little" room was for grades one through four, and the "big" room was for grades five through eight. Each grade had five or six students, so every class had its own row of desks. There was no kindergarten.

My informal "kindergarten" days included helping my mom in the kitchen, setting out milk cartons for lunch, and playing outside with kids from the "little" room during the fifteen-minute morning and afternoon recesses. Sometimes, I also watched the kids from the "big" room during recess. My worst memory was of Willie Castleberry, a fifth-grader, staying outside after recess. Willie and I were standing next to the building, talking, when Mrs. Giesge, Willie's teacher, came out looking for him and was furious. I felt terrible. I thought it was my fault that Willie got into so much trouble. It was a pretty scary experience for a five-year-old. I later learned that Willie got the ruler. He had to put his hands on the teacher's desk, and she whacked his behind with an eighteen-inch wooden ruler.

Every day, Mom, my brother Dan, and I walked the half-mile to school and back home every afternoon. Walking a mile each day for 180 days a year over nine years totals about 1,670 miles, which helped me keep my weight steady. Just think about it: Mom might have walked thousands of miles (although she sometimes got a ride later on). I didn't have to walk barefoot in the snow; however, winters in northern Illinois were harsh seventy years ago.

Early Days

I was born on April 5, 1946, in Highland Park, Illinois, making me among the earliest baby boomers. I was baptized on June 9, 1946, at Santa Maria del Popolo Church in Mundelein, Illinois, where my family had resided for approximately 1.5 years. My godparents were my mother's brother, Gene, and sister, Harriet. In February 1946, my parents bought a house on Bradley Road, a dusty gravel road in Libertyville Township, for $5,000. We moved there in September. They made a $1,800 down payment and financed $3,200 through a mortgage, which they paid off early, securing the title in December. I lived in that house for two years. In October 1948, we sold it for $7,000 as we prepared to move to California. During our trip, we stopped in Colorado to visit my dad's sister, Ruth, and his brother, James, and his family. It was my first time visiting the state, although I don't recall anything. We settled in Garberville, Northern California, before relocating to Palm Springs. My father was briefly on the Palm Springs Police Force until the department realized he didn't meet residency requirements. I still have his police blackjack, a short, lead-weighted impact weapon. With my father struggling to find work, we moved back to Lake Bluff, Illinois, just ten months after leaving.

In August 1949, my parents bought fifteen acres on Bradley Road for $3,000. Our new home was next to the one we had left in 1948. Mom and Dad quickly built a small house with a lot of help from my grandfather, Dan McNeil. The Potawatomi Indians, a long-standing resident tribe, once lived on the land. The Potawatomi were relocated after surrendering all their territory east of the Mississippi River to the US government in the Treaty of Chicago in 1833. They were moved in 1838.

My mother often said that I was related to the Bradleys by marriage, after whom the road was named. It wasn't until years later that I learned my great-aunt, Ellen Ludlow, had married James Augustus Bradley (Gus) in 1879. He was born twenty years earlier on Bradley Road. The road was named after his father, a pioneer farmer from the 1840s. Ellen's parents, Patrick and Mary Ellen (Meehan) Ludlow, were also early settlers in Lake County, arriving from Ireland in 1842. The early settler period occurred just four years after the Potawatomi were forcibly removed from the land.

Our modest house, situated across the road from the old Bradley Farm, was my home until I turned 22. The house measured approximately 25 feet by 25 feet, with an additional half-story above, for a total of about 875 square feet. The first floor featured a living room that also served as a dining area, a kitchen, a three-quarter bath with a shower but no bathtub, a utility area, and one room upstairs. Both the living room and kitchen had knotty pine paneling. My mom, dad, brother Dan, and I shared the upstairs bedroom until I was ten years old. Although winter nights were cold, the chamber pot helped reduce the need to go downstairs for bathroom breaks. Still, my mom had to make that trip! The upstairs had no heating, but an oil-burning heater in the living room provided some warmth and helped dry wet mittens during the long Illinois winters. In 1956, the house was expanded, adding two rooms on the first level and a dormer on the second floor. This remodel allowed my parents to have a bedroom on the first floor, while we gained a utility and storage room, as well as a separate space for our dining table.

After my parents built our house, they had a pond dug to the south of the house. It was a beautiful pond for about fifteen years, but erosion gradually filled it in. During those early days, frogs croaked to signal spring. Then came the Killdeer with their distinctive call, Red-winged Blackbirds on the cattails, and lightning bugs. We had a homemade raft like the one in Huckleberry Finn, and we swam in the pond. In winter, we shoveled snow to skate and even played hockey. In high school, we hosted a few skating parties.

We always had a large vegetable garden. Early on, we raised chickens, rabbits, and ducks. Sometimes, I had to be the axe man (actually, I used a knife), and plucking them was quite an experience. We also had a couple of hogs and many hunting dogs.

About five acres of our property consisted of a mowed lawn that surrounded and extended behind the house—the farthest mowed area served as my baseball field. Surprisingly, mushrooms would grow in late summer at the outer edge of that area. One of my duties was to gather the mushrooms for dinner. I don't recall my mother ever buying them, which made it a special treat.

1950, Our home on the Dusty Road

1951, Dan, Mom and Me at home

1951, Age five, sitting on the picnic table in our yard

1951, Ring, Dad, Me and Dan at home

1954, The Pond at home

Chapter 2: Family

My Mother: Eleanor Seyl McNeil

Mom supported me through my formative years (and I am still in them). She was caring, generous, respectful of others, and hardworking. She allowed me to explore life and make mistakes. I never wanted to disappoint her. However, I often felt that I had let her down because of my poor academic performance in high school. I hated for her to see my bad grades. Still, graduating from Northern Illinois University and earning a master's degree from Adams State College in Alamosa, Colorado, hopefully made up for any disappointment.

Mom was born in 1917, just three months after her father died of a stroke, which family lore says happened while he was operating equipment on their small farm. Her mother, Julia (Carroll) Seyl, managed a household of six children, with the oldest being a sixteen-year-old Joseph. Julia was listed as the farm manager in the 1920 census, but by 1930, at age 52, her role had shifted to doing general work in private homes. It must have been tough. The 1920 census shows her son, Joseph, then 18, working as a file clerk in a packing plant, while 16-year-old Harriet held a similar job at an insurance office.

The 1930 census listed Eugene, 24, as a gardener; Lincoln, 22, as a truck driver; Walter, 19, as a grocery clerk; and my mother, 12, as attending school. My great-grandmother, Julia Alice (Ludlow) Carroll, 87, was also living in the house.

Aunt Harriet recounted how she took the train to Chicago to work for a small wage at a light bulb factory when my mother was a teenager. She saved enough money to buy my mother, who was fourteen years younger, a beautiful dress for a school event. The sisters stayed close all their lives. My mom didn't drive, so nearly every Friday, Aunt Harriet drove five miles to Bradley Road to take my mother to the A&P in town for groceries.

Two of my mother's brothers, Walter and Lincoln, died in the late 1940s, so I never had the chance to know them. However, her other two brothers, Joe and Gene Seyl, lived nearby. Uncle Gene and Aunt Bert built a beautiful house next to Mom's childhood home on land that was once part of the Seyl farm. Meanwhile, Uncle Joe and Aunt Millie lived in Highwood, a town next to Highland Park, where my father grew up, and I was born. Aunt Harriet and Uncle Benny lived in Libertyville. We visited my aunts and uncles at different times throughout the year, and they also came to our house.

The house where my mom was born and raised was on a small farm, less than 4 miles from her great-grandparents' homestead. Her ancestors arrived in Lake County in 1842 from Meath County, Ireland. My mom graduated from Deerfield High School in 1936. She married my dad at St. Patrick's Church in West Lake Forest, Illinois, on September 2, 1939. Hugo Schneider served as the best man, Ruth McNeil was the maid of honor, and her brother Gene Seyl gave her away.

St. Patrick's is where my mother's grandparents, Julia Alice Ludlow and Owen Eugene Carroll, were married in 1868. Growing up, we often attended midnight Mass at St. Patrick's on Christmas Eve.

My mother was listed as a domestic servant on the 1940 census. She worked for wealthy families in Lake Forest, including the Swifts, Armors, Laskers, and others. Tragically, her mother passed away on October 19, 1941, and just twenty days later, my mother lost her baby girl on November 7. Despite these hardships, my brother was born in 1943. The decade of the 1940s ended with the deaths of her brother Walter in 1948 (age 37) and Lincoln in 1949 (age 42).

The 1950 Census listed my mom as living on a farm (our fifteen acres were considered a farm) and keeping house. In 1951, she worked as a temporary cook at Rondout School, earning $3 a day. At that time, she cooked for about 45 students and two teachers; later, as the school expanded, she eventually got an assistant after twenty years. She left this temporary job 37 years later.

Hundreds of children loved Mrs. McNeil, and she had a profound influence on many students' lives over the years. She mentored and cared for the students, and it was an honor to assist with the final lunch preparations, which rotated among the students. The little room ate at 11:30, followed by the big room at noon. After each group finished eating, we would line up outside the kitchen and say, "Thank you, Mrs. McNeil, for the very nice lunch." The students at Rondout School valued her deeply. Many classmates would tell me, "You are so lucky to have Mrs. McNeil as your mom. You must have great meals at home." I was fortunate, and we did enjoy excellent meals at home.

While at Rondout, I would walk to school with my mom, who usually finished her work and returned home by 2:30 p.m. She was always there for Dan and me when we got home from school. She had the same winter and summer vacations as we did.

The lunch program costs $2 per month per student and provided twenty lunches with milk during lunch and in the afternoon. This would provide her with $90 each month (totaling $1,050 in 2025) to spend, along with various USDA agricultural products, such as surplus butter, flour, canned vegetables, cheese, and ground beef. She had to be resourceful. In the fall, she would visit orchards to buy apples by the bushel. She would always roast turkeys for Thanksgiving and Christmas, bringing them to the classrooms so the children could see them.

It seems logical for her to take a job as a cook at the school. She received several ribbons at the Fall Harvest Festival in Deerfield, 1943: a first-place blue ribbon for "Black Cherries" in the Open Kettle category; a blue ribbon for "Corn Cob Pressure Cooker"; and a second-place red ribbon for "Baby Beets Pressure Cooker." Her homemade bread and doughnuts were outstanding.

Mom loved gardening and had many flower beds. My parents' vegetable garden was quite large, featuring a variety of crops, including potatoes, raspberries, asparagus, strawberries, sweet corn, cucumbers, tomatoes, green beans, green peppers, lettuce, radishes, cabbage, and rhubarb. One year, they tried to grow peanuts, but that didn't work out. We also enjoyed honey from our two beehives, straight from the comb.

One year, 22 asparagus roots arrived in the mail. Mom was surprised and disappointed to see how spindly the roots were, but they didn’t let us down. Mom and I planted them in two rows, giving each plant plenty of space. In a couple of years, we had a thriving asparagus bed. In June, we often ate asparagus twice a day. I haven’t had creamed asparagus on toast since then. Later that summer, dinner included sweet corn, onions, tomatoes, green beans, and cucumbers. In August, Mom was busy canning tomatoes, beans, and pickles. Friends frequently dropped by and left with a bag of corn, tomatoes, beans, and maybe a green pepper or two.

Late summer marked the start of berry picking. Mom, my brother Dan, and I would carry two five-gallon buckets and three smaller ones, walking half a mile west across the railroad tracks into the woods, where open areas were filled with blackberry bushes. This area would eventually become my camping spot and later part of the Lake County Forest Preserve. We used ropes or belts around our waists to hold our small buckets, keeping both hands free for picking. When a bucket started to fill, we would transfer its contents into the larger buckets. My little bucket didn't fill quickly because the berries were so delicious. Mom made jelly and froze some of the berries. Frozen blackberries over ice cream became a wonderful winter treat.

I have three vivid memories of my mother and breakfast. The simplest breakfast was buttered toast sprinkled with sugar and cinnamon. Another favorite during winter was oatmeal topped with cream from Meadow Gold Dairy's non-homogenized milk, with a big pat of melting butter in the center and a sprinkle of sugar. The third was what I called the Gold Medal Mother breakfast. It featured chicken livers. In the spring of my senior year of high school, I achieved the third-fastest 880-yard dash time in Illinois. I learned that to perform your best, your blood needed to carry plenty of hemoglobin. So, how do you increase hemoglobin? Iron. A great source of iron is liver. I would wake at 6:30 a.m. to the smell of chicken livers (not exactly appealing). Loads of ketchup made them more palatable. What a sweet, wonderful mother to do that. I'll tell you how that turned out a bit later.

In those early years, we often got new pants and shoes at the start of school. I was lucky to inherit many nice clothes from Jimmy McKay and Stevie Heiser, most of which were from Marshall Field's, a department store in downtown Chicago and Lake Forest. Still, there were tears and worn spots on the knees and elbows throughout the year.

My mother wasn't a seamstress, but she could sew patches on our shirts and pants and darn our socks. Darning socks was a tough job. The heels wore out fast back then. Today, pants often have tears at the knees, but in the 1950s, they weren't considered cool.

Christmas was a joyful time for our family. We had many wrapped gifts; although they weren't fancy, we appreciated them all. It was also a time to be with Mom's siblings, including Uncle Joe and Aunt Milly, Uncle Gene and Aunt Bert, Aunt Harriet and Uncle Benny, and their children. There was love, warmth, and happiness everywhere.

Mom was also my Cub Scout Den Mother. I don't remember exactly how many Cub Scouts there were, but it was probably fewer than six. Once a week during the school year, after school, we had a pack meeting. Mom organized activities for us in our small living room. We played games and did crafts, making gifts for our moms and dads. She taught us the Cub Scout Code.

A Scout is trustworthy, loyal, helpful, friendly, courteous, kind, obedient, cheerful, thrifty, brave, clean, and reverent.

This was the code I experienced in our household. How lucky I was to have such a wonderful mother! She passed away on June 24, 1989, at 71, from lung cancer. She was too young.

My Father: Roy McNeil

During my early years, my father worked as a cement finisher, operated a tape-making machine, and drove an asphalt truck for road paving. As a cement finisher, he was a member of the Carpenters and Joiners Union and later joined the Teamsters Union as a truck driver.

Dad finished grammar school and attended high school for two years. During the Great Depression, his family faced tough times. One summer, he rode the rails with a friend to the wheat fields of Minot, North Dakota, to earn some money. He made $18 a month but had a place to sleep and meals provided. After the wheat harvest, he returned to Illinois.

He was a hard worker, often spending hours in the large garden after dinner on summer evenings. There was a local tavern, Bill's Place (where I would later work), where he sometimes stopped for a beer. He seemed to know everyone, and they all liked him. There was no flash in Roy. He was who he was, and that was good enough for him.

He had an incredible Irish tenor voice. Of course, I always felt embarrassed when he sang. Although untrained, he auditioned for NBC Radio in Chicago in 1934 at the age of twenty. He received a thank-you letter, which I still have, saying they would keep a record of his performance. My Uncle Gene, who had gone with my dad, often said that Dad would've passed the audition if he'd had a few beers. I wish I had a recording of him singing "My Wild Irish Rose," "Danny Boy," or "Toora-loora-Looral" (That's an Irish Lullaby).

He loved the outdoors and grew up hunting and trapping. During the 1930s, in the middle of the Depression, he helped support his family by trapping. He spent long days along the rivers in south-central Lake County, setting and checking traps. It was cold, wet work. Back then, a mink pelt brought good money, as did muskrat pelts, though to a lesser extent. During the Depression, a mink pelt could fetch $10, roughly equivalent to over $200 today.

In the 1960s, he sold raccoon pelts after winter weather stopped asphalt paving. The value of raccoon pelts was about $6 then, which is roughly $65 today. Raccoon pelt prices spiked in the late 1950s, mainly because of the popularity of the TV show "Davy Crockett" from Walt Disney, as baby boomers sought coonskin caps. However, most of these caps were fake, not real. I never owned a coonskin hat myself.

I went hunting with my father many times. We hunted rabbits, pheasants, squirrels, raccoons, and foxes. I can assure you that fox hunting was not done on horseback. I was first taught how to use my dad's Winchester .22, made in 1914, and I later switched to a .410 shotgun. Each fall, Mom and Dad hosted a Harvest Dinner. Dad's friends brought wild game they had shot, so the dinner included pheasant, rabbit, squirrel, raccoon, and sometimes deer, black bear, and wild boar.

Dad had stomach surgery in September 1942 and again in December 1944, though I'm not sure why. I mainly remember the scars on his stomach. His selective service status was classified as 4F. In 1956, our family planned to go to the Shrine Circus at the Medinah Temple in Chicago. However, Dad needed back surgery to have two screws inserted into the vertebrae in his lower back. While Dad was recovering, Dan and I went to the circus with my cousin, Jeanne Siljestrom, and her husband, Bob Sumeriski.

My dad would sometimes play catch with me, but I only remember him going to one movie, *Old Yeller*. He did take me to one sports event, an exhibition baseball game in Lake Forest featuring the Kansas City Monarchs from the former Negro Baseball League.

I still remember the excitement my brother and I felt when we went to the Carpenters Union Hall to meet Santa Claus for the first time. The hall was crowded with kids running around and playing, with sweat running down our faces, and then Santa arrived. We waited in line for what seemed like ages. Finally, I sat on Santa's lap and talked to him. He handed me a brown paper bag with an apple, some hard Christmas candies (which I never liked), and some licorice. What a night! It was a blast!

Dad's back was a problem, so he had to switch from the demanding work of being a cement finisher. He found a job operating a machine that made tape—more details to come. After about six years, he developed liver hepatitis from solvents like methyl ethyl ketone. That required another job change. For the rest of his life, he drove a six-wheel truck for Peter Baker and Son, an asphalt paving company. This meant he didn't work during the winter. And there were no more family summer adventures.

It was a cold, clear Christmas Eve afternoon in 1958, and I was playing with my friend Larry Bennett. He lived near the Print-O-Tape plant where my dad worked. We noticed smoke rising from the building's eaves. We ran as fast as we could toward the plant, where fire trucks were arriving. There was a lot of noise and chaos. The firefighters shouted, hoses were scattered across the parking lot, water streamed onto the building, smoke billowed into the sky, and the fire blazed. It was a frightening moment.

Then I saw a family friend, Eddie Smith. He was a real practical joker. He was talking to another man and said, "I understand Roy McNeil escaped the fire but was taken to Condell Memorial Hospital." I thought Eddie had spotted me out of the corner of his eye and was joking around.

I quickly understood how serious the situation was. Everyone at the plant left on Christmas Eve except for my father and Bob DeWire, the owner. They were testing a new 40-inch-wide tape machine, which was twice as wide as the usual twenty-inch model. The tape's adhesive was very flammable. There had been occasional fires before, but they were always put out quickly. Unfortunately, during testing, the new 40-inch machine caught fire, and the building was soon engulfed.

My dad and Mr. DeWire used fire extinguishers as long as they could, but it was no use. The fire quickly got out of control. They fought the flames longer than they should have. When they tried to escape, the doors were pulled shut by the vacuum created as the fire consumed the oxygen inside the building. At that time, doors in industrial buildings often opened inward rather than outward. With quick thinking, my father broke a large window near a door. The additional oxygen caused the fire to roar, but it also created just enough of a break in the vacuum for them to pull the door open and squeeze out. Since the fire started at the machine Dad was operating, his face and arms were severely burned. The firefighters couldn't save the building, which contained hundreds of gallons of flammable material.

For a brief moment, I watched the fire in awe. Then Larry and I ran a mile along the railroad tracks to my house. Mom was there and knew what had happened. However, no one knew how badly my father had been burned. Within a few hours, the house was filled with neighbors and friends who came to offer their support. Mom held up remarkably well, always seeming as calm as possible.

Mom, Dan, and I gathered around the TV to watch the evening news on WMAQ-TV Channel 5 to find out if there were any updates on the fire. Alex Dreier described the fire and mentioned that Roy McNeil had been injured and taken to the hospital. We waited for him to come home.

Later that evening, Dad came home with bandages on his face, ears, and arms. After resting for several hours, he was determined that we all attend midnight mass at St. Joseph's Church. He sat through the service in severe pain but was grateful to be alive. It was a tragic Christmas Eve, yet it could have been worse.

The day after Christmas, my dad took me to the ruins of Print-O-Tape. I often went with him to the plant in the evenings or on Saturdays so he could finish an order. Now, it was just a twisted heap of steel, broken cinder blocks, and shattered glass. We explored the wreckage and found my father's lunch pail; the thermos inside had exploded. We saw two fire extinguishers: one had melted and lay next to the remains of the large machine, while the other was on the asphalt parking lot where it had landed after my father threw it through the window just before they escaped.

In the 1950s and 1960s, Dad would finish work by 5:00 p.m., and Mom would have dinner ready by 5:30 p.m. During the summer, after dinner, we worked in the garden. But on Wednesdays, I got to watch *Wagon Train*. I often wondered how my father managed to work all day and then tend the garden in the evening.

Before planting our asparagus, we picked wild asparagus along the back roads in early summer. In the fall, we collected black walnuts, hazelnuts, and hickory nuts on the same roads. Since my father grew up hunting and trapping in Lake County, he knew the best nut trees in the area. I spent many winter nights cracking nuts and picking out the meat with my mom. Ice cream with chocolate syrup and black walnuts was a winter favorite.

My dad was the barber at home and did a pretty good job too, cutting my hair since I was six. When I was a high school sophomore with a girlfriend and becoming more aware of my appearance, I had been working for over two years, and I finally splurged on a $1.75 professional haircut in town. I wasn’t at Rondout School anymore; I knew I had to be ready for the big time.

Dad often made sauerkraut in a ten-gallon crock using about 25 heads of cabbage. He would shred the cabbage, salt it, and let it ferment for two weeks. That would last us until after Christmas. I've never tasted better sauerkraut.

Dad was an amateur boxer in his youth, and I have several of his medals. He loved watching the "Gillette Cavalcade of Sports, Friday

Night Boxing." I would watch with him and wanted to try boxing, so I bugged him to get some boxing gloves. Eventually, he gave me the gloves. They were authentic—big and well-padded. My first boxing match was at Johnny Fisher's house, but my boxing career was short-lived. Very early on, Johnny punched me in the nose; it hurt and bled. No more getting hit in the head. The gloves were never used again.

My father had hay fever and asthma, which were so severe that Dr. Peter Vinciguerra would visit our house. It was my only experience with doctors making house calls. He would drink tea made from ragweed and goldenrod, two plants that caused him considerable discomfort. My job was to gather cuttings of these weeds every night from the tall grass and weeds behind my ball field. This helped him find some relief. Sixty-five years ago, there was no Sudafed.

Dad passed away on August 16, 1972, from pancreatic cancer. He was 58 years old. Like my mother, my father was supportive and encouraged me to pursue my interests. I felt fortunate as a young man.

My Brother: Dan McNeil

My brother and I were very different. While my brother loved classical music, design, and art, I preferred sports like baseball and football, as well as outdoor activities like camping. He was two grades ahead of me in school.

He played the cello in his high school orchestra. After graduating, he spent a year studying art at Illinois Wesleyan University in Bloomington, IL. I have no idea why he didn't go back.

In 1967, Dan worked in Deerfield as an illustrator for Kleinschmidt Laboratories, a subsidiary of the Smith Corona Corp. This might not have been the creative outlet he had hoped for. He then turned to cooking.

He was very creative and talented with languages. He studied French in high school and gained basic proficiency in German and Spanish through work. Food played an essential role in his life. He began his journey in gourmet cooking at the Knollwood Club. Initially, he worked with Willie, a German chef, and Pierre, a French chef. He learned to cook and languages at the same time. He once owned and ran his own catering business. He loved cooking, entertaining, and displaying his art collection.

His passion for design led him to the miniature homes industry, where he created detailed miniature houses that typically cost about $10,000. He received a commission to reproduce the Jeffersonian

Reception Room at the U.S. Department of State, which was later displayed at the Palm Springs Museum. I was lucky enough to see it while attending a conference in Palm Springs.

Another project involved recreating the chambers of the United States Supreme Court, both the Old and New chambers. Justice Sandra Day O'Connor led this effort. She wanted the Supreme Court Historical Society to find a way to replicate the two courtrooms. Dan, I, Justice O'Connor, and several other justices attended the unveiling of the replicas, which are displayed in the museum area of the Supreme Court Building.

Dan also built a replica of Thomas Jefferson's home, Monticello. He loved the house and enjoyed recreating it. The project's details were exquisite: paintings on the walls, carpet on the floor, furniture, and everything else included.

Marshall Fields Department Store in Chicago showcased products from the UK and hired Dan to build a replica of Chatsworth House in Derbyshire, England. The home of the Duke of Devonshire has been owned by the Cavendish family since 1549. Dan traveled to Derbyshire to meet the Duke and Duchess and tour the estate. The Duke and Duchess attended the project launch at Marshall Fields, which is considered one of Dan's most notable works.

Dan worked on many significant projects; his primary business involved supplying homes and architectural components to retailers across the country. He often appeared in trade journals.

My brother Dan passed away in December 2001. Just like my father, he was 58 years old when he died. I was deeply shocked by his sudden death. Just two months earlier, he had visited my home in Estes Park, Colorado, to discuss his plans to sell his business and make changes in his life.

Dan's wake was at McMurrough Funeral Chapel in Libertyville, the same place where my parents' services took place. After the service, I took Dan's ashes to Colorado. There were no plans for his remains.

Fifteen years later, I learned it was possible to receive a blessing of Dan's ashes in Nepal. This would be meaningful. Dan had traveled to Kathmandu and was very interested in Buddhism.

I was planning a trek to Everest Base Camp in Nepal and decided to bring Dan's ashes with me. During the first five days of my journey up the Khumbu Valley, I carried Dan's ashes in my backpack, and my thoughts were with my brother and our life together. When we reached Pangboche, Lama Geshe blessed each member of our team and then created a special moment by blessing Dan's ashes. Later that evening, I released the ashes into the river at Pheriche, in keeping with Buddhist practice. It was an incredibly emotional experience for me, and it felt like something Dan would have greatly appreciated.

It was confirmed after his death that he was gay. This revelation wasn't surprising; I regret that he didn't feel comfortable enough to be open about it, which might have given him a better chance at happiness.

As I write this, I am 79 years old. I reflect on the life I've lived since I turned 58. Dan and Dad's lives were cut short.

My Grandparents

My paternal grandfather, Daniel Charles McNeill, was the only grandparent I ever knew. He was born in Campbelltown, Argyllshire, Scotland (1888-1966). His father, Douglas Findlay McNeill (1871-1963), and his mother, Martha Stillers (1870-1943), were unmarried. Shortly before he died, I had a brief visit with my paternal great-grandfather, Douglas, who was born in Kirkmichael, Ayrshire, Scotland, and died in Des Plaines, Illinois. Martha was born in Campbelltown, Argyllshire, Scotland, and died in Oradell, New Jersey.

Daniel McNeill, raised by his grandparents, Elizabeth and Charles McNeill, emigrated to America in 1891 aboard the City of Rome. He arrived in New York and would never see his mother again. At the age of eighteen, in January 1907, he enlisted in Troop L of the 5th Cavalry of the US Army and was stationed at Whipple Barracks in Arizona Territory. Later, he followed in his grandfather Charles's footsteps by working as a contractor in northeastern Lake County.

Note: the second "L" in McNeill was omitted when they moved to the United States.

Daniel McNeil married my paternal grandmother, Emma Nettie Cote, in 1909. Emma was born in Chicago, Illinois, in 1883 and passed away in 1944. Her parents, Frederick (also known as Alfred) Cote (1849-1930) and Lenora Racine (1849-1925), were both born in Quebec City. Alfred immigrated to the United States in 1871, while Lenora did so in 1866. They got married in Chicago in 1873.

My paternal grandmother's family line traces back to Hélène Desportes, my ninth great-grandmother, who was born in Quebec in 1620. She is recognized as the first child born to European parents in Canada (then called New France), according to the Dictionary of Canadian Biography. Her parents, Pierre Desportes and Françoise Langlois, both from Normandy, France, arrived in Quebec in 1619.

Hélène's parents are my tenth great-grandparents. They were companions of Samuel de Champlain, the founder of New France, who established Quebec as a fortified trading post in 1608. During the 1629 British occupation of Quebec, Hélène's family returned to France. After her parents' deaths, she returned to Quebec in 1634 with her mother's sister, Marguerite Langlois, and her husband, Abraham Martin. She married at fourteen, became a widow with three children by age nineteen, and then married Noël Morin, with whom she had twelve children. Their firstborn was Agnes Morin, my eighth great-grandmother. Hélène Desportes died in Quebec on June 24, 1675.

My maternal grandmother was Julia Alice Carroll, born in Deerfield, Lake County, Illinois, in 1876, and she died in 1941. Her mother, Julia Alice Ludlow, was born in Deerfield in 1846 and died in 1935. Her father, Owen Eugene Carroll, was born in Chicago and lived from 1843 to 1884.

Julia married Joseph Anthony Seyl, my maternal grandfather, in August 1899. Joseph was born in Chicago in 1870 and died in 1917. His father, Anton Seyl, was born in Horchheim, Koblenz, Germany, in 1817. He emigrated to the United States in 1852 and died in Chicago in 1885. Joseph's mother, Louisa Dillon, was born in New York in 1843 and passed away in Hot Springs, Arkansas, in 1915.

Unfortunately, I never met my grandmothers, both of whom died in the 1940s, or my mother's father, who died three months before she was born in 1917.

1936, Mom's Deerfield High School Graduation

Mom and Dad

1932, Dad during the wheat harvest in Minot, North Dakota

1939, My parents' wedding at St Patrick's Church, Hugo Schneider, Ruth McNeil, Gene Seyl, Mom and Dad

1958, Dad, Dan, Mom, and me outside St Patrick's Church

1962, Dad with raccoon pelts ready for market

1949, Before my first haircut

1950, With Dad and Dan

1951, With Dan

1953, With my grandfather, Dan McNeil, at home

2000, My big brother Dan

Dan and Chef Pierre at the Knollwood Club

1901, My maternal grandmother, Julia Alice (Carroll) Seyl, was with her first child, Joseph

My maternal grandfather, Joseph Anthony Seyl

Dad's Parents, Emma Nettie (Cote) and Daniel Charles McNeil

My paternal second great-grandmother, Elizabeth (Findlay) McNeil, was 99 years old, and my grandfather, Dan McNeil.

2016, Lama Geshe in the Himalayan village of Pangaboch blessed Dan's ashes and placed a cord around my neck called a *sungdi* for protection and good luck

Chapter 3: Life on the Dusty Road

The Millers' Farm

One of my favorite memories was of visiting the Millers' farm, about a mile south on the Dusty Road. Mr. Miller, who worked nights at the Foulds Macaroni Company, would bring home macaroni scraps each morning for the hogs. I helped toss the lumpy macaroni into their troughs. As I grew older, we harvested corn in early fall. We walked down the rows, tearing the corn cobs off the stalks and throwing them onto a wagon pulled by two draft horses, Blaze and Scout. Blaze was my favorite — friendly, gentle, big, and always happy to eat corn and sugar cubes from my hand.

With a few dozen laying hens at my feet, I would play with the box turtles that lived in a large, round livestock water tank. From the tank, I could see Lonnie, the oldest son, along with Blaze and Scout, plowing the cornfield north of the house, just beyond the hog pens.

Mrs. Miller did all the cooking on a wood stove. I would go to the woodpile and bring back small pieces of wood for the fire. I often watched her candle eggs with a real candle. This was done a few days into incubation to determine if the eggs were infertile and should no longer be incubated. We ate in the kitchen, the warmest spot in the house. In addition to the kitchen, the house had a front room. It's incredible how two parents, three kids, and a grandmother managed to live in that small two-story home. I mention this because I still vividly remember the cold air seeping into the house through the poorly insulated walls. Of course, there was no indoor toilet, but a hand-operated water pump was available in the kitchen.

Next to Miller Farm stood the childhood home of the renowned former resident, Marlon Brando. From 1938 to 1941, Brando attended Libertyville-Fremont High School. In his autobiography, *Brando: Songs My Mother Taught Me*, he candidly admitted, "At Libertyville High, I was a poor student, a chronic truant, and an all-around incorrigible." One of the most infamous incidents from his youth involved him riding a motorcycle through the school hallways, which led to his expulsion.

Howdy Doody

In 1952, I learned we were going to Cynthia Woods's house to watch a TV show. I was confused because I had never seen a television before. My mother explained that it was like watching a movie, but I didn't understand because I had never been to the movies. Four kids and several moms gathered in the room when the screen flickered on —wow! Buffalo Bob Smith started the show by asking, "What time is it, boys and girls?" and they answered, "It's Howdy Doody time." A puppet sang, and our excitement was undeniable! After that, my interest in TV grew. In just two more years, we got our own nineteen-inch Philco TV.

My Dog Ring

Howdy Doody was quite impressive, but he was no match for my dog, Ring. He was a skilled squirrel-hunting dog, my first companion, and my only friend before I started school. He remained so for many years afterward. He pulled my rusty red wagon and walked to school with me. When we arrived, I would tell him to go home. He left reluctantly, but when school was out at three o'clock, he was often waiting for me at the school gate. He was an outdoor dog with a doghouse, not tied up, so he had the freedom to roam. When the temperature dropped below zero, he sometimes jumped up and put his paws on the living room window, signaling that he wanted to come in. He never stayed inside for too long.

My Brush with Greatness

In the summer of 1956, Jimmy McKay and I visited Lake Forest College to watch the Chicago Cardinals' NFL team during their summer camp. At the time, the practice area was simply a football field surrounded by a running track. As we walked along the track, a Cardinal player approached me, picked me up, and held me in the air, asking, "Who are you for?" He wanted to find out if I was a Bears or Cardinals fan. At just ten years old, I hadn't made up my mind, so I replied diplomatically, "Anybody from Chicago." He found that hilarious and set me down, patting my head as he walked away. Jimmy was stunned and asked, "Do you know who that was?" I said no, and Jimmy told me it was number 33, Ollie Matson. Ollie Matson was one of the best players in the NFL, a future Hall of Famer, and a two-time Olympic medalist in 1952. After the 1958 season, he was traded to the Los Angeles Rams for nine players. Since Jimmy was so excited, I got excited too, creating an excellent memory.

Ollie was a truly imposing man; he left a lasting impression on me. Since the Cardinals also held summer camp in a nearby town, I decided the Cardinals were my team. The Cardinals have been around since 1898 and joined the newly formed NFL in 1920. They were one of the original NFL teams. They even played in Comiskey Park, home of my favorite baseball team, the Chicago White Sox. That was a sign.

My new team was struggling with low attendance, so they were sold and moved from Chicago to become the St. Louis Cardinals of the NFL for the 1960 season. There was to be another move in 1988 to Arizona. I was disappointed. However, a new league, the American Football League (AFL), was starting in 1960, and a team in Denver was set to join that season. Since living in Colorado was my dream, I naturally chose to root for them. I loved watching their games on TV, especially the views of Bears Stadium (it became Mile High Stadium in 1968) and the Denver foothills. If I had to lose my team, the Broncos were a great alternative. Go Broncos! More to follow.

Camping with Friends

My friends and I often camped out during the summer. We had beautiful oak forests for camping. These spots were so close to home that we could easily make a quick trip back if needed. Today, they are part of the Lake County Forest Preserves. I have walked in the Forest Preserve several times, and it's nice to relive those nights and days in the oak forest. One camping spot was on our property, south of the house. I had an old World War II pup tent without a floor that I kept set up under a large cottonwood tree all summer. I spent many nights in that ragged tent.

Lying in the raggedy pup tent, I never thought I would sleep on a glacier in Alaska, at Everest Base Camp, high in the Andes in South America, or near Mount Kilimanjaro's summit. My dream was just to someday camp in Colorado's Rocky Mountains.

When I was thirteen and fourteen, my Boy Scout experience was limited because of a tragic accident involving our Scout Master, who lost both legs below the knees while working at the Milwaukee Road switching yard in Rondout. We worked with our assistant Scout Master, who helped us earn merit badges and do some camping. The highlight of scouting was spending two weeks each summer at Camp Ma-Ka-Ja-Wan in Pearson, Wisconsin, 250 miles north of the Dusty Road. I still remember the excitement and uncertainty of leaving home for the first time as I climbed into a bus with two guys from my troop and fifty other boys from Eastern Lake County.

I was in Blackfoot Village in year one and Fremont Village in year two. We slept in tents on platforms, four per tent, and ate in the dining hall. Our activities included swimming, skeet shooting, archery, canoeing, hiking, and overnight treks. We also took part in various crafts and attended merit badge sessions. It was a simple yet valuable learning experience during my last years at Rondout School. Unlike today, there were no zip lines, climbing, rappelling, horses, dirt bikes, sailing, or girls.

1951, My early days at the Miller Farm
I am riding Blaze

2023, The Miller's barn is all that remains 72 years later

1961, My backyard

1959, My pal Ring.

1961, A fresh carpet of snow covers part of our garden

1961, Our small gray house in winter

1967, Fall garden maintenance

Chapter 4: The Rondout School Years

Rondout was an unincorporated railroad town located at the junction of the Chicago, Milwaukee, St. Paul, and Pacific Railroad (known as the Milwaukee Road) and the Elgin, Joliet, and Eastern Railroad (EJ&E). Its motto was "around, not through Chicago," and it was founded in 1887. The EJ&E ran behind our property. Rondout was also the site of the Great Train Robbery of 1924, when the four Newton Brothers carried out the largest train robbery in American history, stealing $3 million (equivalent to over $56 million in 2025). However, they were quickly caught in Chicago. This event later inspired the Hollywood movie *The Newton Boys,* featuring Matthew McConaughey. I mention this because it's a story I heard repeatedly.

Several families from Hazard County, Kentucky, moved between Hazard County and Rondout. They worked for the railroad and lived in shanties owned by the railroad along the north side of the EJ&E tracks in Rondout, which crossed Bradley Road roughly halfway between my house and the school. I didn't know much about Appalachian poverty, but it was clear these families were struggling. Mom kept a large washtub in the furnace room next to the kitchen in the school's basement. Sometimes, she and Miss Thompson, the "little" room teacher, would help wash some of the first and second-grade students. Mom would give them clean clothes. In those early years, Mom always kept a supply of hand-me-down clothes for kids who might need them.

The Lake County nurse visited our school every fall to perform vision tests. In second grade, I learned that children who couldn't read the fourth line from the top of the chart would receive a note sent home to their parents. This note indicated that the child needed glasses. The chart was simple, showing a capital E. Did the E point up, down, toward the windows, or the blackboard? Not wanting to wear glasses, I decided to memorize the letters instead.

By fourth grade, I could no longer pretend. I got the note, and it was the first time anyone realized I couldn't see worth a hoot. Glasses were in my future. The good news was that I could see the blackboard and a lot more. The bad news was that playing schoolyard football and basketball, along with participating in recess activities, meant my frames kept breaking. My father kept them in working order with glue and tape. They were a real hassle. As my eyesight worsened, my glasses became thicker.

Grandfather

My grandfather, Dan McNeil, wasn't a particularly cheerful man; he was often grouchy. He stayed with us during the summers. He would suddenly arrive one day in his '48 Dodge pickup truck with a homemade camper. Instantly, the equilibrium of our little world was disturbed. He lived in the camper during the winters in Yuma, Arizona. He would send us a box of unshelled pecans and Medjool dates. My mother and I spent hours cracking and shelling the pecans. The dates were pitted and ready to eat. My father built a small living space for his father in our barn-like garage. My mother always invited him to dinner, and he would occasionally accept.

He was very thin, had diabetes, and needed to inject insulin every day. His main daily activity was hoeing and pulling weeds in the garden. He did a great job with it and was very protective of his work. This caused significant problems for boys who wanted to play baseball in the backyard. When a ball went into the garden, it was considered a serious infraction. What he did outside of working in the garden was a mystery to me.

But we somehow managed to get along. He did, a few times, come through with a baseball, and he took me fishing on the pier in Waukegan, where we caught perch in Lake Michigan. Back then, it was common to fish from the pier using a "trolley." That practice is no longer allowed at Waukegan's pier, now called Government Pier. It involved a rotating line with many baited hooks. A spider anchor was thrown into the lake, with short fishing lines attached every foot and equipped with baited hooks. Then we would wait. There was a small bell where the line was secured on the pier. When the bell rang, we knew a fish was on the line. We would pull the cord, remove the fish from the hook, rebait the hook, and return it to the water. Setting it up, operating it, and breaking it down was quite a project. My favorite part was digging into the lunch my mother packed for us.

In early summer, he would pick dandelion greens for salads. Google says they are a good source of vitamins, minerals, and antioxidants. They tasted bitter to me. I am sure I unknowingly benefited from the antioxidants.

He led an interesting life, and it seems like a difficult one. Now I wish I had spent more time with him and listened to his stories, such as his experiences in the cavalry and the Yukon. I also wish he had told me about growing up in an immigrant family and being raised by his grandparents while his father lived just a few blocks away.

My Fifth-Grade Evaluation

Our teacher, Mrs. Matson, evaluated each student in the late fall of fifth grade. It's hard for me to picture that ten-year-old boy. Still, some of her insights resonate with my adult experiences. My assessment follows.

> *Now that I have had a little time to get acquainted with your child, you may enjoy having the picture I get of him as he works and thinks among his peers in the classroom. Please feel free to correct me if I have missed some of his best traits, as all of my reactions are subject to the usual amount of human fallibility.*
>
> *Jerry is one of the finest lads I have ever taught. He is a natural leader—creative and tactful—and he really throws himself into every task that involves interacting with his social group. He would rather not work alone, but perhaps he should, simply because the experience of self-discipline would be an opportunity for growth. His classroom work is well done. He is one of the group's most avid bookworms, reports well on his work, and is accomplished in any situation that brings him before the group. He is popular, too, and they always confer honors and responsibility on him first. He offers to help, does tasks without prompting, and generally does very well indeed.*
>
> *Sincerely Yours, Virginia Matson*

I Got the Ruler

As I mentioned earlier, Willie Castleberry was punished with a ruler, and I experienced the same thing myself. Since my mother was present in the building, I tried to stay out of trouble. However, one winter day after recess, I had snow packed into my pant cuffs. While sitting at my desk, I came up with a clever idea to put snow on Johnny Fisher's seat, who sat next to me. He was among the last to return to the classroom. When he sat on his wet, icy desk chair, he jumped up, almost falling out of his chair onto the floor. Mr. Lyon immediately knew I was responsible. He was furious. I was called to the front, leaned over, and placed my hands on his desk as he swatted my behind with a thick eighteen-inch wooden ruler, giving me three heavy whacks—no more, no less. Three was just enough. I learned my lesson: if you're going to put snow on someone's seat, do it far from your own desk.

I Loved Baseball

In the spring of 1956, I was finishing my fourth year at Rondout Grammar School. I turned ten in April, and spring in rural Illinois was usually a little rainy, at least a little soggy. Still, it was time to get outside. The only after-school activity was baseball; it was played with a softball, not a hardball. I wanted to join in.

When there were only a few kids, they played Bounce or Fly. There was a batter and a pitcher, while everyone else stayed in the outfield. The first person to catch a ball on the fly or after the first bounce got to replace the batter. Baseball was for the big kids from the "big" room; fourth graders were not welcome. Bounce, or Fly, was a pretty casual activity. I could join in, since having one more person to chase the ball was helpful.

But the kids in the 'little' room couldn't play during game time. After-school baseball games were only for the guys in the "big" room, along with Judy Kavanis, an eighth-grade girl and a great hitter.

This wasn't a very organized baseball game. The two best players took on the roles of captains and made the team selections from those present. Once the selections were finished, I volunteered to play. They told me I was too small and questioned how I could play since I didn't even have a glove. Most afternoons after school, I kept hanging around, watching and hoping for a chance to play. This went on day after day. I longed to get in and play. Finally, my opportunity came when Jimmy McKay collided with the chain-link fence, bloodied his nose, and had to go home. Johnny Kauffels' team needed a player. Losing a player was tough. Rarely did more than five or six players make a team, and the opposing team always provided the catcher. One player was the pitcher, and the others filled in around him. If there weren't enough players, it was agreed that any ball hit to right field on the fly counted as an out. So Johnny rearranged a few players and told me I could play second base. My big chance! I was in the game!

They doubted I would play much since I had no glove. It didn't bother me because I had always played catch barehanded. As the game went on, I hung in there. A hard ground ball was hit to me, and I dropped it. Luckily, I had time to pick up the ball and throw it to first base for the out. Man, did that sting! I rubbed my hands together to dull the pain and quickly got back to my position. There was no way I was going to let any of those guys think I wasn't tough enough to play with them. My play at second base wasn't too bad for a little guy with glasses. I had my start.

My first official appearance didn't mean I would always play, but as the school year ended, I started playing more often. I believed that baseball was the best part of being in school. Little did I know that someday, Rondout would have a real team competing against other schools, and I would be the coach! I would also become the basketball coach and the de facto athletic director.

My Uncle Gene found a three-finger baseball glove in his barn that summer. He asked me if I wanted it. I said, "Oh yeah." This glove wasn't just old; it was ancient. The leather was dark and cracked. You might say it had a nice patina. It had no padding, and the leather had worn very thin. It was a relic. It certainly wasn't a modern glove, but it was my first. It was too big, so I put four fingers into the little-finger slot. Later that summer, my collection doubled when my cousin Jeanne's husband, Bob, gave me his old catcher's mitt, another relic. Bob was a policeman in Lake Forest and had been a catcher on his high school baseball team.

When I joined the Little League team, my dad and I went to Wells and Copithorne Hardware in Lake Forest, where he bought me a Spaulding Phil "Scooter" Rizzuto glove. The store was owned by my father's Aunt, Annie (Cote) Wells, and David Wells. Annie Cote was my grandmother Emma Cote's sister.

Back Yard Ball Park

Living in the country gave me plenty of space to play baseball, but there weren't many kids to join me. Over the years, my father built a backstop for me in our backyard, which was once a cornfield. With fifteen acres, there was enough room for my ballpark. The backstop was made of four six-foot posts and chicken wire. The bases were burlap sacks filled with straw. I moved several wheelbarrows of dirt to create the pitcher's mound. I used a piece of 2x4 for the pitcher's rubber, and the home plate was cut from plywood.

Most days, I played baseball alone near the house. I would throw a tennis ball against the garage door or toss a baseball over the utility wires crossing our driveway. Sometimes, three or four players joined me, but most days it was just one other player or me. When three players played, one would bat, one would pitch, and the third would stand in short left. When only two of us played, we had a pitcher and a batter. Any ball hit to right field was considered an out. The batter relied on ghost runners to advance around the bases with each successful hit. After three outs, we rotated positions. The hot summer days drained our energy; we drank from the garden hose and kept playing for hours. As we got older, we started batting exclusively left-handed because our hits traveled too far.

Baseballs were scarce; these were the real deal, hard balls, not soft ones. So we had to make the most of the ones we had. After prolonged use, the balls would become soft and mushy, and the covers would start to come loose. At this point, we wrapped the balls with white adhesive tape and kept playing. Over time, the balls accumulated layers of tape, becoming heavier and softer. Sometimes we lost a ball in the weeds, but we never threw one away. The same tape also helped extend the life of our bats when they cracked.

The ball shortage forced us to take drastic measures. Jay Hook was a relative of my Aunt Bert's and played for the New York Mets. Jay was the first pitcher to win a game for the Mets during their 1962 inaugural season. My aunt got him to sign a ball for me, but unfortunately, it had to be sacrificed. I still have the autographed ball, though it's a bit roughed up.

I played Little League in town on the Libertyville Fire Department team when I was eleven and twelve. I got to ride to Foulds Field on a fire truck. We were an expansion team that went winless in our first year; however, we finally broke through with a couple of victories in our second year. My only trip to the hospital until I turned 27 happened when we played against Miller Mercury, and their fastball pitcher, Tom Mellen, hit me in the forearm. It hurt so much that I cried after the game, and my parents took me straight to Condell Hospital for an X-ray. The X-ray was negative, but it still hurt like hell. Besides that, it was a good season, and I was chosen as the starting shortstop on the All-Star team. This was my chance to play in the Little League World Series in Williamsport, PA. We lost our first game to Mundelein 3-0, which ended our run.

I was just twelve when Tom Mellen hit me with his fastball, and neither of us has forgotten it. We became good friends during high school. He was a star on the LHS basketball and baseball teams and one of the friends who camped at the McNeil Nature Preserve. I mentioned earlier that the EJ&E Railroad ran right behind our property. One night after camping, Tom asked, "How can you sleep with the sound of the locomotives throughout the night?" I was somewhat surprised by the question, as I had heard the trains since I was three; I hadn't even noticed them.

I also spent many hours shooting baskets at Tom's house on Johnson Street in Libertyville. He had a 45 rpm record player, and one unforgettable song was “A Quarter to Three” by Gary US Bonds. It was a great song to shoot baskets to.

I took a year off from baseball and then played in the Pony League with the Lions Club team. The games were played at night under poor lighting, and my poor eyesight, even with glasses, eventually ended my baseball career. Playing third base at night with limited vision was nerve-wracking.

I played Boys Club football during my seventh and eighth-grade years. We were the Hornets, wearing green jerseys. I played as an end on both offense and defense. Catching passes wasn't my strong suit because I could only see well with my glasses (no glasses during football). We were champions one year; unfortunately, my small trophy is missing. It was fun, but nothing compared to baseball.

In seventh grade, I participated in my first track meet. Several rural grammar schools were invited to the Oak Grove School Invitational Track Meet, held at Libertyville's old high school track at the Brainerd Building. This event marked the beginning of my career in long-distance running in high school and college, culminating in 1976 at the Fiesta Bowl Marathon in Scottsdale, Arizona.

When I first arrived at Libertyville-Fremont High School, I thought running the mile on the track team would be easy. So, during the fall, I jogged half a mile south on Bradley Road before heading back home. This became my training routine, marking the start of my journey in track and cross-country.

I traded my baseball glove for a pair of track shoes, and then I was shoeless (explanation to follow).

Family Road Trips

On summer weekends, the family sometimes camped by the Fox River. I loved camping and fishing there, but the long road trips were the best. We enjoyed five family vacations exploring different parts of the country. Our trips included a journey through the Great Smoky Mountains, a ride across Lake Michigan on the Milwaukee Clipper to Muskegon, Michigan, on our way to Niagara Falls, two trips to Colorado and South Dakota, and a visit to Michigan's Upper Peninsula.

My first trip was in 1956, when we drove 1,000 miles to Denver, spending two long days along the Lincoln Highway (US 30). Lincoln Highway was the first transcontinental highway across America, dedicated in 1913. This route took us through Iowa, Nebraska, and Colorado's high plains. With gas stops, trucks, and tractors on the two-lane road, our average speed was about 45 miles per hour. The weather was hot and dry, so we kept all the windows down for ten to twelve hours straight. I loved that trip and Colorado. Standing on the steps of the State Capitol with my father and brother—not just any step, but the one marked *one mile above sea level,* the Mile High City—I felt something special. We went camping and fishing, and the cool mountain air was so refreshing and unlike anything I'd ever experienced. I told my mother, "I'm going to live in Colorado when I grow up." On the way back, we visited the Black Hills in South Dakota, where we saw Mount Rushmore, the still-in-progress Crazy Horse Monument, and Badlands National Monument (designated a National Park in 1978). That trip was a real education for me. I was fascinated by the history of the native people and the western expansion in the mid-1800s. Eventually, my dream of living in Colorado came true. The morning after my last class at Northern Illinois University, I drove to Denver to find a job. And I still love road trips.

My First Job

My first paid job was with a commercial photographer named Stephen Hieser, who lived at the southern end of Bradley Road. His daughter, Ginny, was in my first-grade class, which jump-started my brief modeling career. I earned $25 for each shoot. I built snowmen for an insurance ad, posed at a school desk for a Honeywell advertisement, and left footprints on a locker room floor for BF Goodrich and others. That $25 would be worth over $300 in 2025. None of my modeling work remains; however, I still have a photo from an ad my father appeared in for Booth Shrimp (see page 43).

When I was in seventh grade, I got my first real job. Every day after school and on Saturday mornings, I went to Bill's Place Tavern, about half a mile from the school, and then one mile to get home. In the basement, I cleared out the bottle chute of empties, put them into cases for pickup by the supplier, and stocked the beer coolers behind the bar. On Saturday mornings, I collected my $10 and a bag of pretzels. I still love pretzels.

On many Saturdays, after grabbing my $10 bill, Larry Bennett and I would bowl three games at Liberty Lanes, a short distance from the tavern on Rockland Road. We played for 50 cents a game, and the rest went into my savings account at the First National Bank of Lake County in Libertyville.

Leadership on the Fly

In eighth grade, I asked Mr. Lyons, the school principal and the 'big" room teacher (the man with the eighteen-inch ruler), if I could organize a school basketball team. In his deep, jovial voice, he replied, “Sure, why not?” He was skeptical but recognized the importance of his students taking on projects and responsibilities.

I faced two challenges: recruiting a team and finding schools willing to play us. Recruiting didn’t take long; I quickly assembled a six-member team and didn’t turn anyone away.

There was another big challenge: we didn’t have a gym, so all our games had to be played away from home. I needed to find schools with gyms. The principal’s office had a phone, and I got busy scheduling our basketball games during recess.

We were the Rondout Rebels, facing a demanding twelve-game schedule. Our uniforms included blue gym shorts, white T-shirts, and large blue numbers ironed onto the back. Mrs. McCall, one of the few moms with a car, always drove us. The entire team rode in her 1957 Oldsmobile Super 88, made up of six boys and the driver.

We practiced after school in our classroom. We pushed the desks aside, and one team member stood on the three-foot-tall cabinets at the back of the room, holding a box that served as our basket. It was about four feet shorter than the standard basketball hoop, which is ten feet high.

Larry Bennett, my best friend, was a year older than I was and in high school. We went to Libertyville to watch a high school basketball game. The warm-up drills were fascinating. The rhythm and speed of two rows of players doing layup drills caught my eye. My coaching instincts kicked in, and I realized we needed to do this. However, with only six players and one player holding the box, the layup drills never felt as smooth as I had envisioned. Naturally, the box holder constantly moved the box to protect himself from a flying basketball that might hit him in the head.

Most of the schools we played against were small, like Rondout, so they didn't have a gym. Luckily, we could play those schools at the Jackson Gym in the Brainerd Building at Libertyville- Fremont High School. I can’t recall who I had to persuade to let us play there.

One memorable game was against Carl Sandburg Jr. High’s “B” Team in Mundelein. It was a new school with a gym, and we were excited to play in the brand-new facility. Mrs. McCall took us to the gym right after school. As we walked inside, their coach was crossing the floor. He wore cool black Coach shoes, a gray shirt that said "Carl

Sandburg" on it, and a whistle hanging around his neck. He seemed impatient and called out, "Where is your coach?"

I raised my hand and said, "Here I am." He seemed stunned. After realizing the coach was a short kid with thick glasses, he told us to go to the locker room to get ready. I said, "No problem," and we quickly took off our pants and shirts to show off our fabulous uniforms. We were ready! By the end of the season, we had two wins and ten losses, which Mr. Lyons called "all moral victories."

My first theatrical performance was in fifth grade. I played a Native American threatening a colonial family in the major production of "The Inn of the Golden Cheese," which was written by my fifth-grade teacher, Virginia Matson. After that night, my acting career stalled.

Graduation day was in June 1960. My graduation gift was a Motorola 6-transistor pocket AM radio. It was awesome; it even came with a wired mono earpiece.

The only school I had ever known was now behind me as I prepared to start at Libertyville-Fremont High School. Moving from a class of seven to over two hundred students made me nervous.

Rondout School

1954, Third Grade

1955, Cub Scouts

1955, In our driveway with Jimmy McKay, Johnny Fisher. Let's play baseball.

1954, Sitting with Mom in our backyard with the EJ&E train passing behind

1953, Watermelon in the backyard with Dan, Cousins Peggy Maughan and Mike Seyl

In 1956, I was with Dan and Dad on the One Mile Above Sea Level step at the Colorado State Capitol. Twenty-three years later, I met with the Governor there.

1958, Libertyville Little League All-Star Team. I am in the middle row, second from the right.

Large Crowd Sees Rondout Grade School Play

This scene, depicting a home during the colonial days of New England, was a part of a play, "The Inn of the Golden Cheese," presented Friday night by the pupils of Rondout Grade School, Bradley road, before a large crowd [illegible] Linda Evenson, as Peggy Austin; John Koffel, Tom Austin; Marsha Wagner, seated, as Gran Austin; Virginia Heiser, as Sally Austin, a Jerry McNeil, as the Indian. Mrs. Christi Gieseke is principal of the school.

1958, Inn of the Golden Cheese. I am on the right.

1960, Rondout Rebels

June 1960, Rondout graduation

1960, In our living room after graduation with Mr. Lyons. The man with the 18-inch wooden ruler.

1965, Dad in a Booth Shrimp magazine advertisement. Photo by Stephen Heiser.

Chapter 5: High School Years

In the fall of 1960, I started my high school journey at Libertyville-Fremont High School (LFHS). The original building, known as the Brainerd Building—where Marlon Brando once rode a motorcycle through the hallways—was built in 1917. In 1956, the school moved to a new campus. After eight years in a two-room school, transitioning to high school was intimidating. Luckily, in 1960, only first-year students were still using the Brainerd Building, which made it feel less overwhelming. In my second year, students from Fremont Township transferred to their new school in Mundelein, leading to our school's name change to Libertyville High School (LHS).

My home was five miles away from the high school, making transportation a constant challenge. We only had one car, and my mother didn't drive. Every morning, the school bus picked up my brother and me at 7:15 for our 45-minute trip to school. After school, the bus took us back home, but if we had after-school activities that required a ride, we had to find another way.

On our way to school, the bus routinely turned south on St. Mary's Road before turning around in the Adlai Stevenson Farm driveway. Stevenson, known as the "Man from Libertyville," was an Illinois governor and a two-time presidential candidate who was defeated twice by Dwight D. Eisenhower. Tragically, in 1965, while serving as the US Ambassador to the UN, Stevenson suffered a fatal heart attack in London.

A family friend, Joe Robinson, owned a stable on South Bradley Road and was a frequent visitor to our home. Joe advised the farm manager on how to care for the horses at the Stevenson Farm. Joe was at the farm on July 14, 1965, when Stevenson passed away. As a token of appreciation, the farm manager gifted Joe a gold-fringed 48-star flag that had once been mounted on Gov. Stevenson's limousine.

In 1968, Joe gave me the Stevenson flag after I had done some work for him at his home. A few months later, Joe passed away, leaving me with a piece of history.

In my first year at LFHS, October 1960, John F. Kennedy was campaigning for President in town. After giving a speech at Cook Park, his motorcade drove down Brainerd Avenue, right past my English classroom, and we hurried to the window to catch a glimpse of the senator from Massachusetts.

Making a Friend

At LFHS, I knew some guys from Little League baseball and the Boys Club football, which was helpful. However, during my first few months, I was still learning how things worked. With only two classmates from Rondout, I had to find a way to fit in.

When winter arrived, I decided to try out for the track team. For some reason, distance events seemed like a good choice. The Jackson Gym in the Brained Building had a 110-yard track suspended above the gym, with 15 laps to a mile. I started training on my own, even though I wasn't entirely sure what I should do.

Most importantly, I met a guy named Bill Huxhold on the track. He was the class president and had attended Highland Junior High School, where many LFHS students completed eighth grade. Within a couple of years, he and I became co-captains of the track team. We were best friends throughout high school and college, and our friendship has lasted for sixty-five years.

That winter leading into spring, my world expanded. Bill knew almost everyone, and they all liked him, which helped me meet and connect with my fellow students.

That spring, I started dating Judy Cox. It was a typical freshman romance, full of passing notes in class, a few dates and dances, and long phone calls. The phone calls were tricky because we didn't have a private line in our rural area. We shared a line with five other families on Bradley Road. Each home had a unique ring pattern. If I was on the phone with Judy and someone else picked up, I knew we had to hang up. If I didn’t, someone would eventually politely interrupt and ask for the line. Having a girlfriend and meeting new people every day expanded my world.

My academic activities could have been better, and my education at Rondout may have been lacking. If grades were given for interpersonal skills, I would have received an A. The social experience was enjoyable. My fifth-grade evaluation predicted my future in high school. I joined the track team in the spring and had a positive first year at Libertyville-Fremont High School.

During my sophomore year, I was part of both the varsity cross-country and track teams, which further strengthened my friendships, relationships, and confidence. Maybe trading my baseball glove for track shoes wasn't such a bad choice.

Contact lenses

After starting work at Bill's Place Tavern in seventh grade and saving for a couple of years, I bought my first pair of contact lenses for my 16th birthday. At that time, contact lenses were relatively new and didn't suit everyone. My mom questioned my decision to spend $125 on them, as, due to inflation, this amount would be equivalent to $1,305 in 2025. Still, I believed it was a decision worth making. It changed my life; I was no longer called "four eyes" or stuck with Coke-bottle-bottom glasses. As I walked away from the eye doctor's office, I experienced a bright, clear world for the first time in years, once again enjoying peripheral vision.

Anxiety in the fifties and sixties

The Cold War did bring fear and anxiety about the possibility of nuclear war, but we mostly tried not to dwell on it. Living in a rural area with limited financial resources, my family couldn't afford to build or stock a bomb shelter. At Rondout School, we had an early warning receiver and practiced "Duck and Cover." In the event of an attack, I don't think hiding under the desk would offer much protection. Living 30 miles from the country's second-largest city, Chicago, meant it would likely be a target early on.

In October 1962, during my third year at LHS, there were thirteen days of confrontation between the US and the USSR. Tension was high around the school, and students were aware of the potential for nuclear war and the threat of imminent destruction. The US imposed an arms blockade that restricted Russia's ability to deliver offensive missiles to Cuba. This period was the most unsettling of the Cold War. The threat of nuclear war felt very real—it seemed like it could happen, and the world might come to an end. Then it was over, and we went back to being teenagers.

On November 22, 1963, during an early afternoon geometry class, I heard over the school intercom that President Kennedy had been shot and died. The rest of the school day was canceled. Everyone remembers exactly where they were when they heard the news. After leaving the school building, with very little said, I rode with Terry Langworthy to

McDonald's and sat in his car with my 10-cent orange drink and 15-cent hamburger. We were both speechless. We felt devastated. Suddenly, our world was shaken once again.

First Car

At sixteen, I bought a 1948 Chevy for $40. It had a manual transmission; the emergency brake didn't work; and the gas gauge was broken. It also had a floor starter and a hand throttle, an early version of cruise control. Still, I could travel to school, work, and home all week for just $2 in gas, with enough left for one or two dates on the weekend. When the starter didn't work, I had to park on a hill and roll down to pop the clutch. The following summer, I sold it to a landscaper, a fellow employee at the Knollwood Club, for $25.

My next car was a $125, 1953 Chevy Bel Air with a Powerglide automatic transmission. It had its quirks; sometimes, the lights would go out briefly when I pressed the bright light button on the floor. One time, after a basketball game on a cold January night in Crystal Lake, 25 miles from LHS, the lights failed. I found myself stranded on icy roads, following the team bus back to Libertyville in the winter darkness. My '53 Chevy served me unfaithfully throughout high school, followed by the '58 Chevy Bel Air during college.

In the 1960s, owning a car involved getting new license plates each January, which had to be attached to the vehicle by the end of the month. Illinois winters were harsh, often bringing cold, windy weather with temperatures frequently dropping to ten below zero. The plates needed to be mounted on both the front and rear, but rusty bolts and nuts made this challenging, creating a memorable experience.

Friends and Fun

I had a wonderful girlfriend for two years, starting in my sophomore year: Dorothy Smith. She attended Highland Junior High, was our class secretary, and excelled in her studies. We had a great relationship. Unfortunately, I dreamed of living in Colorado, but I am not sure she felt the same—young love at its best.

Connecting with classmates like Bill and Dorothy felt like a stroke of luck. I often felt out of place as a kid from out of town. Most of the class had been together in junior high for at least two years, and some had been together since first grade. I was fortunate to bond with classmates who were leaders in various aspects of school life. This truly made my high school experience exceptional and unforgettable.

I dated a few friends during my senior year, but none of the relationships were serious. I attended all the major events, like the homecoming dance and prom.

During my high school years and afterward, I was busy working, studying, and spending time with my three best friends: Bill Huxhold, Kent Morgan, and Danny Fohrman. Danny, one of the smartest kids in the class, became a rheumatologist. Bill pioneered the field of geographic information systems and has written many books and articles. Kent became an executive at an insurance company. Hanging out with these three was a wise choice. Kent owned a boat, making water skiing a great summer activity after work, along with all-night poker games at Danny's home. Bill was more into sports, so we went to Cubs and White Sox games at Wrigley Field and Comiskey Park. We also saw the Chicago Blackhawks at the Chicago Stadium. Then there were road trips to Colorado, California, Arkansas, and Michigan. I'll share more about those later.

I also provided LHS football and basketball scores to the Chicago Tribune. Although I didn't receive any pay, I was given a press pass, which allowed me free entry to all LHS away games. I needed to call in the score quickly after the game for the next day's newspaper.

Track and Cross Country

I had some success with both the track and cross-country teams. I served as the captain of the cross-country team during my junior and senior years, and co-captained the track team with Bill Huxhold in my senior year.

In the spring of 1961, during my first year on the track team, I realized that jogging a mile on the Dusty Road wouldn't turn me into a long-distance runner. The training was tough, and my muscles were sore for the first time in my life. My father knew how to handle aching muscles. We went down the Dusty Road to Joe Robinson's stable, and Joe gave us some horse liniment. Well, if it's good enough for Joe Robinson and Adlai Stevenson's horses, it's good enough for me. It worked, but it had a strong smell. Sometimes, our house smelled just like a horse stable.

In my senior year, I became the Lake County 880-yard dash champion, finishing in 1:59.0. This achievement set a school record, and I proudly appeared on the state honor roll with the third-fastest time in the state. The qualifying time for the state meet was 2:02. Unfortunately, an injury to my Achilles tendon sidelined me for a while, causing me to miss qualifying for the state finals by just .8 seconds. My mother's chicken livers could not overcome an inflamed Achilles tendon.

My track events included the 880-yard dash, the mile run, and the mile relay. The 880 was always the second event, giving me time to recover before running the mile. However, the mile relay was the last event and followed immediately after the mile. My role was to anchor the relay, which gave me a few more minutes to recuperate from the mile. An unusual aspect was that I often ran barefoot in both sports; the idea was that having less weight on my feet would result in faster times. I was the team's top scorer for two years, earning steak dinners with Coach Hodgson at George Diamonds Steak House.

During winter, I trained on local bridal paths that wound through hardwood forests and back roads. For competition, I often entered Amateur Athletic Union (AAU) sanctioned races at Chicago's Washington Park. In a 10,000-meter race, I faced competitors like Jim Ryan, the first high school athlete to run a mile in under four minutes, and Tom O'Hara, who once held the record for the fastest indoor mile at 3:56.6. We used the locker rooms at the nearby old Stagg Field at the University of Chicago, which was the site of the metallurgical laboratory where Enrico Fermi created the first nuclear reactor for the Manhattan Project. It was designated a National Historic Landmark on February 18, 1965, but not because I used the locker room.

I was elected president of the Letterman's Club (LHS Athletes Club) during my senior year. We organized a fun donkey basketball game between club members and faculty, which proved to be an excellent fundraiser for our project: building an athletic events board on the school grounds facing West Park Ave. We also hosted Goose Tatum's All-Stars (Harlem Magicians). Goose Tatum was a member of the Harlem Globetrotters for eleven years before leaving to create his own traveling basketball show. It wasn't the Globetrotters, but it was a close second.

At graduation, I was surprised to receive a Citizenship and Community Service Award from the Veterans of Foreign Wars (VFW), which also awarded me a $50 savings bond. The bond helped cover my $127 second-semester tuition at Northern Illinois University.

Work During High School

After working at the tavern for a few years, I started working at the Knollwood Club. I briefly caddied there during the summer after eighth grade, but I wasn't really fond of it. Luckily, I was asked to be the "grill boy" at the club pool snack bar, where I cooked hamburgers, hot dogs, and grilled cheese, and made great milkshakes, earning $400 a month. In later years, my high school friends Bill Huxhold and Tom Pfenning also worked at the snack bar.

I worked several seasonal jobs at the club for three years. When the pool closed, I worked in the clubhouse, washing dishes, scrubbing pots, and polishing and buffing the floors. My brother was the assistant chef, and I was the pot scrubber.

In the fall and spring, I worked in the Men's Locker Room (the sanctuary for the rich guys). I polished shoes, parked cars, vacuumed, tended bar, and cooked. On busy days, a fellow worker and I would shine over 400 pairs of shoes. I polished the shoes worn by Sam Snead (the famous golfer) and by Otto Kerner (while governor of Illinois, before he went to prison for mail fraud).

During the summer on Mondays, I played golf for free on Knollwood's fantastic course. Later, when I had to pay $5 to play on a poorly maintained public course, I stopped playing golf.

During the winter months of my last two years of high school, I worked at the Village of Libertyville's Butler Lake ice skating park. I patrolled the ice like a lifeguard on skates. When the ice cracked and became uneven, we cut holes and used a pump and a fire hose to flood the skating area. Afterward, we scraped the ice with a Jeep blade, and I swept it using a Ford tractor with a rotating broom. We did this on weekend nights, often until dawn. I also proudly finished third in a speed-skating event. That little trophy is long gone.

I also worked at Center Pharmacy during my last two years of high school, where I stocked shelves, checked new inventory, swept up at closing, and made deliveries. I did not get to fill prescriptions.

1960, Fishing in Cache la Poudre Canyon River, Colorado

1960, Mom and Dad in Poudre Canyon, Colorado

1963, I attended prom with Dorothy Smith.

1963, My living room

1963, with Mom on prom night

1963, Christmas in our knotty pine living room

1963, My home

Governor Adlai
Stevenson's Limousine
Flag 1949-1953

1963, This LHS cross-country race was finished on the track, barefoot.

1964, Overtaking Lee Clark from Waukegan High School to become the Lake County 880-yard dash champion.

Chapter 6: Travel with Friends

My grandfather was a wanderer; he was born in Scotland, raised in Illinois, and traveled extensively across the country, even venturing as far as the Yukon. My father undoubtedly enjoyed traveling, and that love was passed down to me. Luckily, my best friends in high school shared a passion for travel. I remember trips with Larry Bennett, Danny Fohrman, Kent Morgan, and Bill Huxhold. When I was sixteen, I had the incredible opportunity to be trusted and supported on a 2,000-mile round-trip journey to Colorado. And that was just the beginning.

Colorado 1962

My first trips to Colorado were with my family in 1948, 1956, and 1960. Our family took vacations most summers while I was growing up. However, when I was fifteen, Dad contracted hepatitis while working at Print-O-Tape, which forced him to find a different job. After that, our summer vacations ended.

In 1962, when I was sixteen, my father suggested that Larry Bennett and I take my ‘48 Chevy to Colorado to visit my aunts and uncles. I spent that summer preparing for a late-August trip, working hard to save money. We were looking forward to being in the mountains and fishing.

We were excited about the trip, so we painted "Pikes Peak or Bust" on the back of the car, even though we had no intention of actually going to Pikes Peak. However, before we left, Larry’s parents were worried that the '48 Chevy might not be suitable for a 2000-mile round trip. They insisted we use their 1956 Ford station wagon instead—lucky us!

The interstate highway system was still under construction, so we traveled on two-lane roads. We drove directly to Denver on US 30, a 22-hour trip. Just before reaching Wheatland, Iowa, Larry passed a farm tractor pulling a wagon, but crossed a double yellow line after passing. We were stopped by the police and issued a ticket. The officer explained that the spot was dangerous and that a girl had been killed there the previous year. We followed him into town and waited at the magistrate's house. As we sat in his front room, we feared we might have to go to jail.

When we discovered the fine had exceeded $100, we were shocked and couldn’t afford to pay it. Considering inflation, that amount would have increased to over $1,000 by 2025. Fortunately, the magistrate promptly reduced the fine, allowing us to pay $30 before continuing our journey west. In 2025, $30 would be equivalent to $318. We had inadvertently fallen victim to a small-town speed trap of sorts; the local authorities were simply trying to generate revenue.

Another memory involved a life-threatening experience. In Nebraska, the seat was folded down in the station wagon while I napped. Larry began yelling, and grass flew past the car windows. He was passing a truck hauling a trailer when the truck tried to pass the car ahead. This forced Larry off the two-lane highway and into the weeds. We were lucky that there wasn’t a ditch where we left the road, or we could have been killed.

We enjoyed our visit with Uncle Jim and Aunt Eva, as well as our time with Aunt Ruth and Uncle Eldon, fishing and camping at Lake Granby. Afterward, we headed to the Black Hills in South Dakota, where we parked the station wagon by the side of the road for the night. It was a great spot as the sun was setting. But oh, the mosquitoes! It was a sweltering August night, and the mosquitoes were so bad that we couldn't roll down the windows. Daylight couldn't come soon enough; at first light, we headed to Deadwood, Mt. Rushmore, Crazy Horse, and the Badlands. We slept on the ground at the Badlands and then drove all the way home.

Porcupine Mountains Michigan 1963

Kent Morgan and I drove my '53 Chevy to Porcupine Mountains State Park in Michigan's Upper Peninsula, where we camped and hiked for a week. When we arrived, we stopped for lunch at a roadside table. Just as we finished, a young black bear wandered into the picnic area. Realizing our lunch was suddenly over, we started putting everything in the trunk. The bear, however, was determined to find food. We had a tin of homemade chocolate chip cookies, and Kent cleverly threw one to distract the bear while I loaded the car. We were afraid Mama Bear might show up. It took a while to get everything packed, and about half a tin of cookies was essential for ensuring our safety.

Spring in Arkansas 1964

During spring break in 1964, my senior year at LHS, Danny, Kent, Bill, and I planned a trip to the Lake of the Ozarks area in Bill Huxhold's family car. The day before we left, Bill and I took part in the Oak Park Indoor Relays, one of the country's largest indoor high school track meets. Two other friends from the meet, Don Johnson and Jack Welu, wanted to join us on our trip, so we ended up with a car full of six guys and camping gear for five days. There was a ten-inch snowfall overnight, but we headed out anyway. When we arrived at the Lake of the Ozarks, in Missouri, we found it so cold that we decided to go further south to the Buffalo River in Arkansas. It was still very cold. Kent was sleeping by the fire when he accidentally set his sleeping bag on fire. Danny saw ticks for the first time, and Jack knocked my hot dog into the fire. Gas was 26 cents a gallon, the lowest price we had ever seen. It was cold, crowded, and created great memories.

Colorado/Mesa Verde National Park 1964

In the late summer of 1964, Danny Fohrman and I went to Colorado to visit my aunts and uncles, though they didn't know we were coming. One Friday morning, we arrived early and slept in the car outside 3419 S. Fairfax St. in Denver. My aunt was a bit surprised when she looked out the window. It was a quick visit; we went fishing with Aunt Ruth and Uncle Eldon, and they took us to dinner at the Golden Ox on Colfax Ave. That was pretty exciting for two broke kids. This was seven months after the Beatles had appeared on the Ed Sullivan Show, and I was a big fan. At dinner, Uncle Eldon said, "There is a lot of excitement now, but I can guarantee no one will remember them in five years." Sixty years later, and the Beatles have not been forgotten.

Before heading to Mesa Verde, we climbed Pikes Peak, which rises to 14,115 feet just outside Colorado Springs. We hiked the Barr Trail with our limited gear: sleeping bags (no sleeping pads), two large cans of Welch's Grape drink, candy bars, and a few donuts for breakfast. After a hard night on the rocks, we got an early start to the summit because we had a long day ahead. We accomplished this—my first peak over 14,000 feet. Worn out, we decided to hitchhike down and got a ride in the back of a pickup truck.

Our next stop was Mesa Verde National Park in the southwestern corner of the state, 340 miles from Colorado Springs. The last 22 miles from Route 160 were on a narrow road leading to the park headquarters and services. It had been a long day, and we didn't realize how slowly those final miles would pass. To our surprise, the only available service upon arrival was a small, single-room cabin selling limited supplies for campers. On a tight budget, the cheapest item was a can of Campbell's Beans and Franks — that would be our dinner. We shared it equally, counting the small franks; there were thirteen, so we split one in half. We didn't bother counting the beans.

After visiting Mesa Verde, we headed north to Grand Junction along US Highway 550, famously known as the Million Dollar Highway. This scenic route connects Silverton and Ouray and was initially built as a toll road in 1880. The highway offers breathtaking views that gave it its name. Our itinerary then took us to the Black Hills, which included Mount Rushmore, the Crazy Horse Memorial, the Badlands, and Wall Drug. The Crazy Horse Memorial started in 1948, and I first visited in 1956, returning five times to see the progress. In 2003, I hiked up to the memorial arm, where I could see the carving up close. It's still unfinished in 2025.

We also made a brief stop at Carleton College in Northfield, Minnesota, where Danny would soon start his studies. After a two-week trip covering over 3,000 miles, we returned to Libertyville.

California 1965

A twenty-one-day trip across America cost $123 ($1,250 in 2025 dollars). Early that summer, Bill Huxhold, Danny Fohrman, and I thought it would be fun to travel to Redondo Beach, California, to visit Bill's girlfriend, Mike, whom he had met during his first year at Washington University in St. Louis.

Early in the summer, we felt desperate about how to travel 2,000 miles to California. We came up with two great ideas—either hopping on a freight train or getting paid to drive someone's car there.

We started with a freight train idea, but it turned out to be a bad one. One Saturday night, Bill, Danny, and I climbed into a boxcar near my home on the EJ&E tracks. We sat inside for a while and then realized it wasn't going anywhere, which was probably a good thing. Sitting in a boxcar is a reality check. LHS produced some talented people, but this wasn't our best moment. We also placed an ad in the Waukegan Sun Times offering to drive someone's car to California. No luck.

Dan's parents owned Center Pharmacy in Libertyville, and they let us use the store's 1961 Chevy station wagon. It was in good working condition.

As plans came together, my time in Colorado would be limited. So, I decided to leave four days earlier, and they could stop in Denver to pick me up. Great idea, but how was I going to get to Denver? I saw an ad in the Waukegan Sun-Times looking for a rider to Denver to share gas. Wow! There you go. I was nineteen years old and heading to Colorado with a total stranger. After Tom, the driver, visited my parents, they felt he was not a serial killer. So now, I had to work hard, make money, and enjoy the summer.

Tom picked me up at 6 a.m. in mid-August, and we drove straight to Denver. Although Interstate 80 was not yet finished, some sections had been completed, and construction was still ongoing. Much of the trip followed US 30, also known as the Lincoln Highway. We completed the journey in about 22 hours. Driving through the night in Nebraska, I enjoyed the scent of freshly mowed alfalfa and the glow of the dehydration equipment, which transformed it into pellets for livestock feed.

We arrived at four a.m., so it wasn't an ideal time to start a visit. Tom dropped me off at the Colorado State Capitol. I had arranged to spend a day with Bill's school roommate, Art Ziporan. Later that morning, I called Art, and he picked me up; I stayed with him for a night in Aurora before heading to Aunt Ruth and Uncle Eldon's for a short visit.

Later that week, Bill and Danny picked me up, and we headed to California on US 6. We left Denver in the early afternoon, traveling through Glenwood Canyon and Glenwood Springs before reaching Grand Junction by early evening. It was my second time on this road, and it was spectacular in the evening light. Little did I know that I would someday work for the state of Colorado, live in Grand Junction, travel through the canyon, and get paid for it.

We were eager to reach California and planned to drive straight through to the Pacific Ocean. In Grand Junction, US Route 6 merged with US 50, often called "the loneliest road in America." We took turns driving every few hours. Around midnight, I was driving on a desolate stretch of highway in Nevada while Danny slept in the back and Bill sat in the passenger seat, talking to keep me awake. Suddenly, a loud bang came from under the hood, and the car seemed to lose power. I quickly pulled off the highway and shut it down. Neither Danny, Bill, nor I knew what might have gone wrong—maybe a blown rod, a gasket, or something else entirely! It was past midnight, and we were in the middle of nowhere, surrounded by total darkness. What on earth were we going to do? If we kept driving, we might damage the engine.

We knew very little about cars, so we did nothing. We waited for a vehicle to pass by—and one did! The guy stopped to see if he could help. He looked under the hood, then went back to his car and opened the trunk, which was packed with automotive tools—a real mobile auto shop! We had found the right guy! He took out a tool and unscrewed our damaged spark plug (the porcelain had exploded). After reinserting the spark plug, he told us it was safe to drive and advised us to follow him to the next town to find a replacement.

Unfortunately, Danny had left us before the guy stopped. He decided to hitchhike back the way we had come. We later found out that he had trouble getting a ride until he chose to limp in the middle of the road. Finally, a Mormon family picked him up. We had no idea where he was.

Without Danny and needing a spark plug, we followed our new friend to the outskirts of a small town, where a seemingly abandoned pickup truck was parked among tall weeds.

It was just starting to get light, so no stores were open yet. He "borrowed" a spark plug from the pickup truck. "You guys need the spark plug more than this guy does."

As daylight broke, we returned to the last place we had seen Danny. On our way, another car approached, and Bill saw Danny's head inside. We were finally reunited, and with a new spark plug, we kept heading west. And it was still my turn to drive.

On our first night in San Francisco, we slept on Baker Beach, right next to the Presidio and not far from the Golden Gate Bridge, which turned out to be prohibited. We hadn't noticed the "No Camping" sign until morning. After that, we drove down Route 101 to Redondo Beach to stay with Bill's girlfriend. She took us to SeaWorld (she snuck us in through the employees' gate), Disneyland, and the Lighthouse jazz club on Sunset Boulevard, where I saw a man over seven feet tall—Lou Alcindor (Kareem Abdul-Jabbar). He was entering his first year at the University of California, Los Angeles (UCLA).

Then, we took a quick trip to Tijuana for some serious shopping, which included a wooden chess set and wooden Don Quixote figures. On our way home, we traveled along Route 66, known as "The Mother Road" and "The Main Street of America," which spans over 2,400 miles from Los Angeles to Chicago. Due to car trouble, we stopped in Las Vegas and then spent the night at a campground near Lake Mead. After that, we drove straight through to Libertyville—a trip across America in twenty-one days for $123.

Isle Royale National Park 1966

Before starting my third year of college, Bill, Kent, and I visited Isle Royale National Park, a remote island in Lake Superior. The island was mainly wilderness with no roads, but it was home to many wolves and moose that roamed freely.

We boarded a national park ferry in Copper Harbor that departed for a three-and-a-half-hour trip to the island, arriving at Rock Harbor. It took a couple of days of hiking and camping to reach West Chicken Bone Lake, where we stayed for several days. Since we had no tent, we slept in a three-sided shelter.

Ode to Chicken Bone Lake
By Jerry McNeil

As the sunlight turns to grey
And water begins to darken
Stillness is broken
The flight of a bird
The wisp of the wind
The sound of nothing

Chicken Bone Lake was a remote, peaceful spot, except for the wolves' howls at night. We fished and hiked during our stay. The lake had too many fish, which stunted their growth. The park ranger told us to discard the uneaten ones onto the bank instead of throwing them back. We followed his advice, and the next morning, we saw that the wolves had enjoyed a fish dinner, thanks to three boys from Illinois. However, one downside of the lake was its warm water, which teemed with leeches and was unsuitable for drinking. Sixty years ago, we didn't have water filters and relied on the local water source. Bill took a quick dip and ended up with several leeches—quite unpleasant! One day, we made a five-mile round trip to fetch cool water from the McCargoe Cove inlet of Lake Superior. We spent our last night at Daisy Farm Camp. It was time to go home. Running low on food, we gathered thimbleberries, mixed them with Bisquick, wrapped the dough around sticks, and roasted them over the fire. We looked forward to returning to the mainland for cheeseburgers. The next morning, a small Park Service boat arrived to take us back to Rock Harbor, where we would catch the ferry to Copper Harbor, where cheeseburgers awaited us. They were so good—better than thimbleberries and Bisquick on a stick.

1963, Pikes Peak, Colorado

1965, I was on my way to Michigan's Upper Peninsula with Kent Morgan in my '53 Chevy Bel Air.

1965, With Danny Fohrman, Bill Huxhold, back from California

1966, With Bill Huxhold, Kent Morgan in Isle Royale National Park, Michigan

1989, With Bill Huxhold, Kent Morgan, 25th LHS Reunion

Chapter 7: After High School

Peter Baker & Son

In 1964, I spent the summer working for Peter Baker & Son, an asphalt paving company where my father worked. My job involved emptying gravel from rail hopper cars onto a conveyor belt, which was then piled on the ground for pickup and transport to the asphalt batching plant. It was a hot, dusty job, but I earned $4.40 an hour, which was great.

The minimum wage was $1.25 an hour, so I was doing well. I could save enough for most of the year while attending Northern Illinois University. I was on the cross-country team at NIU. There was no scholarship, but I got to work several nights a week, staffing the field house for minimum wage. So, how do those wages compare to those of 2025? $1.25 is equivalent to $12.90, and $4.40 equals $45.39. I was paid at union scale, but I did not have to join the Teamsters Union.

Getting back to my dusty job, I started at 7:00 a.m. by oiling and refueling the Caterpillar D7 tractor, which I used to move the railcars. Then, I secured the cars to the tractor to position them for unloading. Once the car was over the drop spot, I climbed onto the hopper car, cranked the brake, and chained the hopper door before opening it to let the gravel flow onto the conveyor and form a pile on the ground. The gravel would drain for about twenty minutes while I rested in the shade or moved other railcars. Afterward, I climbed into the hopper car to shovel any leftover gravel through the open door and onto the conveyor belt. The wind blew up through the exit hole, blowing dust into my face. Each car had two hoppers.

After unloading a series of cars, I had to chain them to the D7 tractor and tow them to a track scheduled for pickup in a day or two. Each railcar weighed about 220,000 pounds when full and around 65,000 pounds when empty. This has haunted me in nightmares for decades. The track had a slight grade, allowing the cars to roll slowly. As they moved, I would climb onto a railcar and crank the handbrake to stop them. In my dreams, I would turn the handbrake, but I could never fully stop the cars.

They would gain speed and eventually tip over, with me still on top, trying to stop them. Cold sweats were sure!

College

In the fall of 1964, I enrolled at Northern Illinois University in DeKalb to pursue a career as a teacher and coach. Gilbert Hall, the oldest men's dorm on campus, became my new home. That first year was a significant adjustment from LHS and home, as my new school had 11,000 students, and I hardly knew anyone. Joining the cross-country team helped me transition into college life.

Tuition was $127 per semester, equivalent to about $1,310 in 2025 currency. In my second year, I lived off-campus at "Ma Brown's," a large brick three-story Victorian house with a dozen other students. There was a kitchen in the basement, and I cooked my meals to help manage my expenses. My roommate, Rick Schwartz, was the evening manager at McDonald's. They closed at 10 p.m., and employees could take any unsold hamburgers or cheeseburgers. The cutoff for cooking more burgers was 9 p.m., assuming there would be very few leftovers. At 8:45 p.m., Rick would start a big batch of burgers so the unsold ones would end up at "Ma Brown's." It was a treat.

Halfway through the second semester, my parents helped me with grocery money. DeKalb was an hour and a half away from Libertyville, so I sometimes made the trip. Naturally, when I went back home, Mom would send food back with me. One of my favorites was stewed tomatoes, made from her homegrown tomatoes, along with green peppers and onions. A quart of Mom's stewed tomatoes and a bag of white rice would last me almost a week.

Classes were tough, and my study skills were weak. During first-year orientation, we learned that only about one in four students would graduate. English composition was often seen as the course most likely to cause students to fail. The good news was that I passed, but I unfortunately earned a "D." This grade meant I had to pass a proficiency test before becoming a senior. Naturally, I waited until the last chance before my senior year to take the test. How foolish was that? I studied and got some tutoring before the exam and passed. If I had failed, I would have had to sit out a semester before retaking it. I just barely avoided that. During the second semester of that first year, I enrolled in a course on the History of Western Civilization. One day in class, I was inspired to write a poem.

History is so wonderful
It is so very fine
But when it's time to study it
My thoughts are those of wine
I go to my bottle and open it
I sip a glass or two
And before you know it
My studying it is through
After another glass or so
I know that I will flunk
But all that I can say is
Who gives a damn? I'm drunk!

The second year was quite stressful. I started each day with a quick breakfast, then took a mile-long walk from Ma Brown's to campus. There, I attended classes and often ate just a Snickers bar for lunch because I couldn't eat much before cross-country practice. I worked at the field house until 9 p.m. Afterward, I walked back to Ma Brown's and cooked rice with my mom's stewed tomatoes. And there was a chance for McDonald's hamburgers if Rick was working. In late October, I injured my ankle and visited the Student Health Center. There, I unexpectedly ran into a student I knew but hadn't seen since the previous year. Her reaction upon seeing me was concern for my health. She noticed that I looked thin and exhausted, and she suspected I was unwell and needed medical attention. I assured her that I was in good health and that my injury was just an ankle sprain. I hadn't realized I had lost weight or appeared depleted. The combination of cross-country running, Snickers bars, and rice had taken its toll.

During that second year, I sank into deep depression, with severe headaches that persisted into my sixties. Focusing on my studies became difficult, leaving me stressed and unmotivated. One foggy December night, I was walking alone near Ma Brown's, feeling overwhelmed by my inability to concentrate. A halo from a single streetlight through the mist intensified my sense of disconnection from happiness, and this brief poem came to mind. More about depression later.

Alone on a Foggy Night

Friends are near
I am not a part
I walk alone
Through the night
I am myself
A dream fulfilled
And through the day
I am what I am not

During college, I wrote a collection of poems titled "Yellow is the Sun, Golden are its Shadows." I shared it with my Aunt Harriet, who said, "These seem a little depressing." She was so right! Unfortunately, the collection was lost, and no one has bothered to look for it. Though I wasn't a dedicated student, my perseverance helped me graduate. It took five and a half years because I changed majors and minors and took a semester off due to poor grades. I earned a Bachelor of Science in Education with a major in Physical Education and minors in Business Education and History. My student teaching included business education at the university school, physical education, and coaching football at George Washington Junior High in Aurora, Illinois. I initially wanted to be a teacher and coach, but after student teaching, I realized I needed more real-world experience before starting my career. Doubting my abilities as an educator, I decided to work for a while before becoming a teacher. However, I never became a classroom teacher. Still, I found my teaching skills invaluable as an administrator. My time at NIU proved to be very beneficial.

NIU Running

I performed well on the NIU cross-country team. Training with my older teammates, who seemed mature and knowledgeable about competitive running and college life, proved to be valuable.

In my sophomore year, I made the varsity team. One of our early meets was in Macomb, where we competed against Western Illinois University and Illinois State University. We traveled in two NIU station wagons and stayed downtown at the US Grant Hotel, enjoying meals in its dining room. Not knowing the ordering rules, I followed the advice of upper-level team members that we could choose anything from the menu, so I picked a lobster tail. I treasured those road trip meals. When we returned to campus, we received a $5 certificate to dine at a local restaurant—another meal I didn't have to prepare.

My barefoot running went well until I raced against Loyola University in Lincoln Park, Chicago. During warm-up and while familiarizing myself with the course in shoes, I saw some broken glass and thought I could avoid it. But as more glass patches appeared, I knew there was no way I could avoid them. That was the moment I realized it would be a shoe day. But we still beat Loyola.

I took my first airplane ride at age twenty during my junior year in college. The track team traveled to Kalamazoo, Michigan, to compete in the Western Michigan Relays. I was scheduled to run the half-mile as part of the two-mile distance medley. We first took the team bus to O'Hare Airport, and I was so nervous about the upcoming competition that I had to find a restroom urgently. When I finally located one, I was shocked to learn that the toilets required a dime to unlock the stall door. Not having a dime, I was grateful when a kind stranger came to my rescue with ten cents, and disaster was averted.

Fraternity

I pledged Sigma Alpha Epsilon and lived in the house for a year. SAE at NIU was a fun and positive group without any extreme antics. We held dances, played on intramural sports teams, participated in community projects, competed in Greek singing contests, and built great friendships. In one Greek singing competition, we were singing the Battle Hymn of the Republic in four parts. After practicing for six weeks and sadly without my father's voice, my last-minute instruction before our competition was to lip-sync. On the upside, one brother tutored me on writing an English composition to pass the competency test. Thank you, Bob!

Music Events

For many baby boomers, the Beatles and the British invasion were captivating. I first heard the Beatles in mid-December 1963 while driving with Bill Huxhold east on Highway 176 at the St. Mary's Road junction in my 1953 Chevrolet Bel Air. When "I Want To Hold Your Hand" was playing on the radio, I was instantly drawn to the song and asked Bill who was singing it. He replied, "The Beatles," as if I had just returned from a trip to the moon.

Bill Huxhold and I saw the Beatles on August 12, 1966. They started their final fourteen-date tour with two concerts at Chicago's International Amphitheater. We sat in the balcony for the evening show. Bill remembers the deafening screams that made it nearly impossible to hear the singing. I recall it as a fantastic concert. The Remains, Bobby Hebb, The Cyrkle, and The Ronettes performed before the Beatles. When the curtain rose, just three guys with guitars stood at two microphones, with Ringo on the drum kit. It seems so simple compared to today's multimedia concerts, which often include pyrotechnics. It was an incredible show for just $5.50 a ticket. In 2019, I had the chance to visit Liverpool and step into a bedroom where a couple of teenagers, John Lennon and Paul McCartney, wrote love songs that changed the face of popular music. I walked down Penny Lane and stood at the gates of Strawberry Fields. These boys were relentlessly inventive and experimental. Their words and music had a profound impact on me when I was a teenager, and they continue to do so.

Since those early years, I have had the privilege of seeing Paul McCartney several times and Ringo Starr twice, each concert with his All-Star band. The tickets for these events were quite expensive, well above $5.50 in 1966.

In 1968, Joan Baez was at the peak of her career. I joined 14,000 others at Ravinia Park to hear her perform the classic folk songs of the 1960s. During my high school and college years, I had the chance to see performances by several well-known artists, including the New Christy Minstrels, Peter, Paul and Mary, Al Hirt, Chad and Jeremy, the Zombies, the Association, the Chad Mitchell Trio, and the Mamas and the Papas (I later met Michelle Phillips while we were on a TV talk show). Also, during a trip to California in 1965 with my friends Bill and Danny, we enjoyed seeing Mary Wilson of the Supremes at Disneyland and Cannonball Adderley at the Lighthouse on Sunset Boulevard in Los Angeles.

Bob Dylan's concert at Ravinia Park on June 17, 1964, was an unforgettable experience for my friends Bill, Kent, and Geoff Batchelder, as well as for me. We had just graduated from high school, the folk craze was in full swing, and Bob Dylan was emerging as a superstar. However, he wasn't a superstar yet. We paid a few dollars to sit on the grass at Ravinia Park, but we could have easily bought seats in the covered pavilion for a few dollars more. Still, we were pretty frugal. We could hear Bob Dylan but not see him. Surprisingly, the pavilion was only half full.

The concert started, and we enjoyed the summer evening sitting on the grass. After a few songs, it began to rain. Dylan immediately asked everyone on the lawn to come inside and stay dry. Although we were already wet, we quickly took him up on the offer and jumped over a gate to find seats. The crowd now filled every seat, aisle, and space.

It was an exhilarating moment, but then his guitar string snapped. That shouldn't have been a problem at that kind of venue, but it was. Dylan called out to the audience, asking if anyone had a spare string or guitar. To everyone's surprise, including Dylan's, a teenager walked up to the stage and handed his guitar to Dylan. He continued to play the borrowed guitar for the rest of the concert. That sixteen-year-old was David Lauterstein, who proudly blogs about Bob Dylan using his guitar back on June 17, 1964.

I had the privilege of watching and listening to Dylan, the future Pulitzer and Nobel Prize winner, up close, using a borrowed guitar and a harmonica harness around his neck, singing "A Hard Rain's a-Gonna Fall," "The Times They Are a-Changin'," and "Mr. Tambourine Man," along with fifteen of his early songs.

Work During My College Years

I worked various jobs to support myself through college. As I mentioned earlier, tuition was $127 per semester, plus the costs of books and living expenses. My earnings from the previous summer and work during school breaks helped me financially get through most of the spring semester; after that, my parents provided support. Here are some of the jobs I held during my college years:

- Emptied railroad hopper cars loaded with gravel for the Peter Baker & Son asphalt paving company.
- Pumped gas and repaired truck tires at Phillips 66 in Rondout.
- Worked as a groundskeeper at Art Baker's estate, who owned Peter Baker & Son.
- Built concrete foundations for homes and replaced curbs and sidewalks in Lake Forest.
- Coached fifth-grade basketball at St. Mary's School in DeKalb.
- Washed dishes at the Sigma Sigma Sigma sorority from Monday to Saturday. A fraternity brother, Dave Kilmer, prepared the meals. I received six dinners and $15 each week.
- Worked the night shift during school breaks, manufacturing printing rollers for newspaper presses.
- Worked for a landscaping company.

- Donated blood regularly at $15 per pint.
- Staffed the NIU Field House during the evenings.

1965, NIU Cross Country

1966, Hitting the books

1966

1967, Sigma Alpha Epsilon fraternity

1966, Heading into the first turn

NIU Harriers Bunched

1966, A barefoot NIU race

1966, I lived at Ma Brown's House in DeKalb for two years.

Chapter 8: Marriage and Children

Marriage

I met Bonnie Jacobson on a blind date in February 1966 during my second year of college. She was a freshman. I had tickets to see the Ramsey Lewis Trio, but didn't have a date. My friend John Peterson from the cross-country team said he knew someone from his hometown of Lockport whom he could call. He made the call, but she wasn't in the dorm. Her roommate, Bonnie, answered; she was also from Lockport. John asked her, and she accepted the invitation to see Ramsey Lewis.

We dated for two and a half years before getting married in 1968. For a year, we lived in a one-bedroom apartment near the campus in DeKalb, paying $95 a month. Bonnie earned a degree in Early Childhood Development in 1969 and started working at a school in Aurora, Illinois. That fall, I completed my student teaching at George Washington Junior High, also in Aurora. By the end of that semester, I had finished my studies at Northern Illinois University.

The morning after my last class, I drove to Denver to look for a job. My dream was starting to come true. We moved to Colorado in January 1970 and enjoyed camping, four-wheeling (also called Jeeping), and exploring ghost towns from the gold and silver mining regions. We moved often, bought a new home each time, and returned to Illinois whenever we could. Luckily, Bonnie was a good letter writer who kept our families updated about our lives.

Bonnie and I separated in late 1982. We have stayed friends and continued to support our children.

In 1984, I married Trish Hogue, whose maiden name is Patricia Wentworth Chase, born in Palmer, Massachusetts. We lived in Alexandria, Virginia, with Trish's daughter, Allison. More about this later.

Children

Jenny was born in Alamosa, Colorado, on December 18, 1972. She has eight children: Cody, Sawyer, Bailey, Noah, Emily, Tyler, Josh, and Ruby. Cody is married to Monica Martinez, and Bailey has a daughter named Saylor, who was born in 2025. They all live in the Sarasota, Florida area.

After leaving Alamosa, we moved to Colorado Springs, Pueblo, and Grand Junction.

In late 1978, while living in Grand Junction, we adopted siblings Susan and Patrick Martinez. The following year, I was assigned to the Denver office, prompting us to purchase another house in Arvada, a Denver suburb.

Susan was born on April 24, 1971, in Denver, and she currently lives in Newport News, Virginia.

Patrick was born on July 28, 1972, in Denver, and he has a son named Cristiano. They live in San Antonio, Texas.

On August 1, 1982, Juli was born in Arvada. She has four children: Ben, Hailey, Will, and Lucy, all of whom live in Las Vegas, Nevada.

Trish's daughter, Allison Hogue, was born on January 3, 1971, in Washington, D.C., and she is married to Richard Floisand. They have two children: Evan, born on December 31, 2003, and Anja, born on December 10, 2005. They live in Seattle, Washington.

1968, With Bonnie

1995, Juli, Jenny, Patrick, Susan and Allison

2002, Jenny, Allison, Patrick, Susan, Juli

Chapter 9: Life in Colorado

Getting Started

In January 1970, I registered with the teacher placement office at the Colorado Job Service in Denver, hoping to find a teaching position. I briefly sold life insurance for John Hancock before accepting a job as an assistant office manager at the Denver Feed Company. My work schedule consisted of nine-hour days and alternating Saturdays, totaling 45 hours one week and 54 hours the next. My starting monthly salary was $400 with no benefits. After a few months, my salary increased to $450. Although the pay and opportunities were limited, it was a valuable experience.

During my early months in Colorado, I was notified to report for a physical exam after my college draft deferment ended. The Vietnam War was ongoing, with US troops there since 1965. A few years earlier, my friends Bill Oskilanec from NIU and Tom Edgren from LHS had been killed in action. My military service would shape my future. I went to the New Customs House in Denver, expecting to pass the exam, but I failed the vision test at station number ten. It was clear I was not fit to serve. My poor eyesight, along with my glasses and contacts, has always been a part of my life.

Bonnie and I lived in a two-bedroom apartment at 51 Washington St, Denver, where the rent was $150 a month. During our first few months, we bought a Jeep CJ5 with a ragtop, removable doors, a fold-down windshield, and no radio—a modern version of the World War II-era Willys Jeep. We often camped on summer weekends when I had Saturdays off. Bonnie was a junior underwriter at an insurance firm, working five days a week. We enjoyed exploring Jeep trails, Colorado's ghost towns, and learning their history. I recall researching at the Denver Public Library's Western History section and learning about the Ludlow Massacre during the Colorado Coalfield War of 1913-14. I never imagined I would one day speak on behalf of Colorado's Governor Lamm at a Ludlow Massacre memorial event.

In late summer, we went to Grand Junction, thinking it might be a better place to live. I visited the Job Service Office to explore opportunities, which turned out to be limited, and I was encouraged to take the Colorado Civil Service exam. I took the exam in Denver as soon as I could.

Stearns-Roger Corporation

Aunt Ruth's close friend, Chuck Hartman, was the corporate secretary at Stearns Roger Corporation and approached my Aunt to ask whether I would be interested in a field accountant position at the home office. The position paid $600 per month, and I was eager to accept, even though I had completed only two semesters of accounting at NIU.

The corporate office had a formal dress code, requiring coats and ties, and strict adherence to break schedules. My supervisor, a 25-year veteran of the company, was demanding and expected his staff to have the same level of knowledge as he did. While he was generally lenient with me, some longer-serving employees often faced loud reprimands.

The first compliment I received was when I told my boss I was leaving. He appreciated my work and said he regretted that I was going. An encouraging word earlier would have helped. But I was ready to move on.

State of Colorado

In December, I was offered a teaching position in Springfield, Colorado, which is in the southeastern corner of the state near the Kansas border. Because Springfield was far from the mountains, I turned down the offer. Soon after, I was offered a job as an employment counselor at the Colorado Division of Employment, Alamosa Job Service Office.

After six months at Stearns Roger Corp., I was ready to leave my accounting job behind. The move took me from Denver to Alamosa, a town in south-central Colorado about a five-and-a-half-hour drive away. Situated in the San Luis Valley at 7,500 feet above sea level, Alamosa offered a new adventure for Bonnie and me. Before leaving, we visited a pet store in Denver and picked out a cockapoo puppy, which we named Moffat. She quickly became a vital part of our lives.

I started my job in Alamosa in February 1971, a year after moving to Colorado, earning $628 per month. To obtain certification, I needed to either earn a Master's Degree or complete 30 graduate credits in Psychology and Counseling. Fortunately, Adams State College was in Alamosa, which made evening classes convenient. I enrolled for the spring 1971 semester. The state funded my tuition and books, provided I committed to working for them for five years. In two and a half years, I earned my Master's Degree. It was quite an achievement, considering I was a poor student in high school and as an undergrad.

The Alamosa Job Service was located at the corner of State and Main, where the town's only stoplight was. The office was furnished with Army surplus furniture. My desk chair was wobbly, tilted, and had no arms. I was told a destruction order had been placed on my chair the week before I started. I managed to get another two and a half years out of it.

During my years in Alamosa, while balancing work and studies, I served on the Alamosa County Youth Services board. I coordinated the Alamosa Jobs for Youth summer program and also served as the External Vice President of the Alamosa Junior Chamber of Commerce (JC). The JCs raised funds by placing US flags in front of downtown businesses on holidays and selling fireworks around the Fourth of July. We set up a temporary fireworks booth on Main Street, and since there was no competition, our business thrived for two weeks. As External VP, however, I had to manage the stress of storing thousands of dollars' worth of fireworks in our garage for six to eight weeks before the sale started. I was always worried that the fireworks might explode in the garage and destroy our home.

In the 1970s, the travel per diem for state employees was $14. Mileage reimbursement was ten cents per mile. When I went to Denver for training, I stayed at Motel 6. The cost was $6, and if you wanted to use the TV, it was 25 cents to get the key to unlock it. Motel 6's slogan was, "We will leave the light on for you," but that would cost an additional 25 cents (joke). That left $8 for three meals. Sometimes I stayed with my Aunt Ruth Veirs in Denver or Aunt Eva McNeil in Longmont. Since receipts weren't required, free lodging meant money in my pocket.

In the early years of my state employment, all my travel was to Denver for training. The Department's main office was just three blocks south of the state capitol. It was easy to walk to the Capitol, where I admired the murals, walked the halls, and stepped into the legislative gallery. I never thought that one day I would be in that gallery listening to Governor Lamm deliver the State of the State address, knowing he would include some remarks I had contributed to his speechwriter.

Pursuing a Master's Degree

When I studied at Adams State College in 1971, it was not yet a university as it is today. My master's practicum supervisor was also a runner. My final college race was against Purdue and Ohio State in Lafayette, Indiana, just before I turned 22, marking the end of my collegiate running days. At 25, while living in Alamosa, I started running again for myself. I rediscovered my well-worn copy of *Run, Run, Run* by Fred Wilt, a book I received while running at NIU. This book served as my running Bible, with chapters covering various topics in long-distance training, curated by Fred Wilt, an FBI agent in Indianapolis. While I received solid coaching throughout high school and college, I also learned training strategies and self-trained during the off-season. *Run, Run, Run,* along with Runner's World magazine, provided the most up-to-date training information in the late 1960s.

While reeducating myself on training for long-distance running, I read a chapter by Leonard Graves Edelen. When I mentioned this to Lorraine Jones in our office, she replied, "Oh, you mean Buddy, who teaches at the college!" At first, I thought she was joking, but she explained that Buddy had come to Alamosa to prepare for the 1968 Olympics in Mexico City. The US Olympic marathon trials were held in Alamosa because of its high elevation. Buddy was a faculty member in the psychology department at Adams State College. I was eager to follow up since I studied in that department.

Oh my gosh, Buddy taught at the college! In 1963, he set a world record in the marathon. This remarkable achievement made him the first American to hold the world record since 1925. After winning the 1964 US Olympic Trials marathon by nearly twenty minutes, an unfortunate injury led to a disappointing sixth-place finish in the 1964 Olympic marathon in Tokyo.

It was an honor to meet him, and we began running together. Although I never took a class with him, he became my master's practicum supervisor. For several years in the early 1970s, we ran countless miles, sharing memories and making new ones. His accomplishments continue to impress me. After graduating from the University of Minnesota, he moved to England to teach and compete in European races. He set the American marathon record in Fukuoka, Japan, in 1962, with a time of 2:18:57. Then he set a world record of 2:14:28 at

Britain's Polytechnic Marathon on June 15, 1963. He ran the original marathon course in Athens and also competed in Moscow and the Czech Republic. Edelen was the first American to break the 30-minute barrier for 10,000 meters. He even had the privilege of meeting Queen Elizabeth and, of course, enjoyed many pints of Guinness.

Buddy was a humble, thoughtful, and modest man—an outstanding ambassador for the world of track and field. I've read his biography, "A Cold Clear Day," by Frank Murphy, three times. He was inducted into the National Track and Field Hall of Fame. Sadly, he died of cancer in 1997 at age 59.

Comprehensive Exam Time

By May 1973, after nearly two and a half years, I had completed all my coursework and submitted my master's thesis proposal. Due to my full-time job as a counselor and attending night classes, I chose to take extra courses instead of completing my thesis; the only remaining step was to pass the comprehensive exam. The night before the exam, my office organized a welcome summer evening picnic on the Conejos River south of Alamosa. I remember feeling conflicted about not being home, studying.

After taking the exam, the day of reckoning finally arrived; it was time to visit Dr. Marvin Motz's office. My academic advisor would give me the results.

Before I share the outcome, let me tell you about Dr. Motz. He was a towering man, standing 6'9", which made him stand out in any crowd. He was an excellent teacher, advisor, and motivator, known for his use of humor like no one else. He had been an All-Star on the ASC basketball team in the mid-50s, and in 1963, he was inducted into the ASC Hall of Fame. Marv was a psychology professor and served as Adams State College's interim president twice. In 1981, he founded the Humor Academy at ASC and lectured across the country and in Europe for 15 years before retiring. He was a favorite professor and made a significant impact on me during my postgraduate studies.

The big reveal: I'm heading into the office of someone I deeply respected and whose opinion I valued. I was nervous. Reflecting on my academic successes and failures, I knew this would be an important moment. In a serious and concerned tone, Dr. Motz told me he was disappointed with my comprehensive exam results. Oh SHIT! Then he said that in a class of twenty-five, I ranked 12th. Well, that didn't seem too bad. Then he shared his thoughts on my future in psychology and counseling. He said, “Jerry, you are intelligent and motivated. In my opinion, you could continue your studies and pursue a PhD.

Wow! That was really amazing. No one had ever said anything like that to me before. He continued, “As I see you, you not only could pursue a PhD but need to.” Please wait a moment; he’s explaining what he thinks I need personally, and he believes that is to continue my education. Honestly, being in 12th place didn't bother me, but the other stuff was overwhelming.

I had great respect for Dr. Motz. I understood that I needed to take his assessment seriously. Bonnie and I discussed what the future might look like if I pursued further education. I felt special after hearing Dr. Motz's evaluation. I obtained the graduate school catalog from Northern Colorado University and tried to visualize the steps needed to earn a PhD. How could we afford it financially? What would I do afterward? How did I view my previous academic experience, and how would that influence my pursuit of a significant goal like a PhD? As the weeks after graduation passed, I began to doubt my ability and desire to achieve that goal. However, motivated by Dr. Motz, I realized I needed to do more with my education in guidance and counseling than work as an employment counselor at the Job Service Office. I wanted to engage in serious counseling.

My master's thesis proposal evaluated new inmates at the Lathrop Youth Camp, a Colorado Correctional School in Walsenburg, during their intake and release processes. The purpose was to capture a snapshot of the boys' self-concept when they first entered and again upon release to see whether it had improved or declined. The study would use Q methodology, a technique developed by psychologist William Stephenson, which is used in psychology and social sciences to study "subjectivity"—people's viewpoints. It assesses a person's progress over time and examines how individuals think about specific topics. This research prompted me to consider a career in corrections.

While working and attending night classes, I served on the board of the Alamosa County Youth Services Bureau with Emilio Martinez, the senior probation officer for the San Luis Valley, and Carlos Lucero, an attorney who later became a judge on the U.S. Court of Appeals for the Tenth Circuit. In discussions with them, both believed that a good next step for my counseling career would be to work at the Colorado Correctional Facility for young males in Buena Vista.

Since I was already employed with Colorado Civil Service, I hoped to transfer to the Department of Corrections. Since no formal positions were posted, I sent a letter of interest to the Human Resources Director at the Buena Vista facility, including references from my two contacts in Alamosa. It was an initial effort on my part. However, as summer progressed, other events occurred. Pursuing a job with the Department of Corrections fell lower on my priority list, and my dreams of earning a PhD faded.

Late in July, while I was still considering the PhD, my boss, Hoyt Williams, called me into his office to inform me that the office was being downsized, and I would be transferred to Colorado Springs to serve as an Employment Counselor in the Work Incentive Program (WIN). Bonnie and I had two weeks to report to the Colorado Springs office. We put our house on the market and headed to Colorado Springs to find a place to live. We found a three-bedroom tri-level house in Northeast Colorado Springs. On the upside, I would be working with welfare participants and managing a caseload of 80, which would give me more opportunities to utilize my counseling education.

My career in the Department of Corrections never took off because I did not receive a response to my initial letter. Ironically, eight years later, I became the director of a state employment and training program that funded initiatives in the Colorado State Prison. Part of my responsibilities involved visiting the prison to evaluate the effectiveness of the vocational training I managed.

The Eight-Year Journey

When Bonnie and I arrived in Alamosa, we rented a small house for about six months before buying a three-bedroom home on 2.5 acres west of town for $15,500. This was the first of five homes we purchased over the next eight years as my career took us from Alamosa to Colorado Springs, Pueblo, Grand Junction, and finally Denver. Bonnie was a champion throughout all the moves. I often had to commute home on weekends during the transitions, leaving her alone during those weeks. There were financial pressures related to buying, selling, and securing bridge loans and mortgages. This journey took me from working as an employment counselor in 1971 to becoming the Director of Colorado's Office of Rural Job Training in 1978.

In August 1973, I was transferred to Colorado Springs, where I worked with welfare recipients in El Paso County. At that time, I held two side jobs: I worked as a bartender at the Rocky Mountain Kennel Club dog track in Colorado Springs, licensed by the Colorado Racing Commission, with evening and Saturday shifts. I also substituted as an instructor at El Paso Community College, where I taught Marketing. Although the WIN office staff was excellent, some people at the central office in Denver seemed indifferent toward the people we served. I worked hard and actively looked for other opportunities. Soon, an opening for the Director of Social Services in Teller County, just west of Colorado Springs, became available. After completing the written and oral exams, I ranked first, and the Board of Commissioners' chairman offered me the position. However, I hesitated to accept because of the responsibilities involved with child protective services, and taking the job would mean leaving the Colorado Civil Service. Ultimately, I decided not to accept.

Soon after, the Colorado Division of Employment and Training opened an office in Pueblo for the Southern Area. Unexpectedly, I was offered a position as an Administrative Staff Specialist in the WIN program at the new Southern Area Office. This was a temporary appointment. When the Civil Service Commission posted the position, I would need to compete for it. I started immediately and commuted 50 miles each way. This continued for six months until I was officially hired for the role.

My job in Pueblo started in August 1974. After spending Christmas in Illinois, I returned to find my position had been cut again. The good news was that the Comprehensive Employment and Training Act (CETA), a federal program, had expanded to the Southern Area, and I was selected to lead it. This was a great opportunity, and I was in charge of implementing a new program. I held this job for about a year, but then another shakeup happened. Merlin Smith, assistant manager of the Pueblo Job Service Office and a senior employee whose position had been eliminated, bumped me from the CETA role.

Luckily, I was able to return to my previous job with the WIN administrative team. Going back to my old role after managing the CETA program for a year felt like a step backwards. However, my year of CETA administrative experience led to an offer for the CETA Coordinator position at the Western Area Office in Grand Junction. This program had a much larger budget and covered a broader geographic area, including 21 counties on the Western Slope and two Indian reservations.

In March 1976, I started working in Grand Junction. Until we sold our house, I commuted from Pueblo to Grand Junction for five months, returning every weekend. The drive was 250 miles each way, and during March and April, the roads were often icy and snowy, especially when crossing the Continental Divide at Monarch Pass, which is 11,311 feet above sea level. In Grand Junction, we bought a new two-story, four-bedroom home. Our front porch offered views of the sandstone cliffs and monoliths of the Colorado National Monument, along with breathtaking sunsets over the Colorado Plateau. To the east of our home across the Grand Valley was the Grand Mesa, the largest flat-topped mountain in the world, dotted with more than 300 alpine lakes. To the north, the sandstone Book Cliffs stretched over 200 miles across Utah and Colorado. Grand Junction was a great place to live, as it was the largest city between Denver and Salt Lake. The weather was pleasant, the orchards were plentiful, and we were just an hour from Ouray, the gateway to the San Juan Mountains. With a population of 35,000 and located 250 miles from a major metropolitan area, it was the go-to spot on the western slope for whatever you needed. My office was on the 7th floor of the Valley Federal Savings building, the tallest building within a 250-mile radius. From my office window, there was a great view of the Bookcliffs. I often joked that on windy winter days, I could see Utah blowing by.

My job required nearly monthly trips to Denver, a five-hour drive. Flying was an option, but Frontier Airlines' Convair 580 propjets, which have both jet engines and propellers, provided a rough ride over the mountains. Additionally, with a stop in Montrose and circling over Stapleton Airport, flying wasn't much faster than driving. The best option was to take Amtrak to Denver and then fly back. The train journey followed the Colorado River through the Grand Valley and Glenwood Canyon, passed under the Continental Divide via the Moffat Tunnel, and offered views of the majestic Rocky Mountains. My coworker, John Wilson, and I often caught the train at 1 p.m., enjoyed dinner on board, and arrived at Denver's Union Station by 8 p.m. It was an enjoyable experience; we flew home afterward.

FBI in My Office

One spring morning in 1977, an FBI agent walked into the Western Area CETA office in Grand Junction. He wanted to speak with the person in charge, which was me. He entered my office and sat across from me, introducing himself as Agent Lyons of the Federal Bureau of Investigation.

He said he was following up on reports that a senior official in the Western Area CETA office had illegally diverted CETA funds to an activist group in Delta County. This claim shocked me. As the highest-ranking official, I was unaware of any illegal transfer of CETA funds.

He had a specific organization in mind. I reassured him that we had contracts with them, reviewed time cards each month, and that reimbursements depended solely on those results. I invited him to review our records. He said he might need to do that later. He stressed the seriousness of these allegations. I felt unsure about what to say or do to prove my innocence. He also mentioned reports of unrest in the mountains of East Delta County, suggesting that CETA funds might be supporting the unrest, and expressed serious concern. After about thirty minutes, Agent Lyons left the office, saying he would return if necessary.

The accusation cast a shadow over my evening. I felt shocked and anxious; what if I had been wrongly accused of a crime? How could I prove that this report wasn't credible? I was scheduled to fly to Denver the next morning, and I worried so much about these allegations that I decided to seek guidance from the Department Headquarters. I tried to get some rest.

The Grand Junction airport was small, so I quickly navigated through the terminal and found my seat. To my surprise, Agent Lyons walked down the aisle. As he passed, he nodded. Seeing Agent Lyons again piqued my curiosity and made me wonder what was happening.

I felt rattled during my flight to Denver. I hadn't done anything wrong, and no one at Headquarters had heard of any allegations or inquiries from the FBI. The uneasiness from that experience lingered with me for weeks. I never heard another word from anyone. Years later, I shared this story with a friend, Jeff Wein, who had served as the CETA director for the City and County of Denver. Jeff had a good laugh at my story. He mentioned that Agent Lyons had been in his office around the same time on a similar fishing trip. There were some cases of CETA funds being misused nationwide, and Agent Lyons might have been trying to catch someone off guard. I haven't seen Agent Lyons in over forty years, but I do keep my eyes open.

Moffat and the Ranch Exit

This story follows a brave, clever, yet anxious cockapoo named Moffat. Bonnie, Jenny, and two foster children, Hannah and Sara, along with Moffat and me, were on our way back to Grand Junction from Salt Lake City. It was early fall in 1977, and covering about 280 miles took roughly five hours, which meant we needed an emergency pit stop. With over an hour remaining, I took a Ranch Exit off I-70. These exits, which aren't connected to any towns or businesses, are marked “Ranch Exit” and rarely see traffic, providing a private spot for the children to go potty. After a brief stop, we resumed our journey and arrived home around 6 p.m. It was a bit hectic. After unloading, checking the mail, enjoying a Sunday night dinner, getting the girls ready for bed, and a short period of relaxation, it was bedtime for everyone. Moffat usually slept at our feet or underneath the bed. However, this time, she wasn’t on the bed when it was lights out. Bonnie said, “I don’t think Moffat is here. Did you let her in?” I couldn't remember if I had. I was about to open the back door for her when we suddenly realized Moffat hadn’t come home with us. She had been outside the VW bus while we loaded the three girls, and we lost track of poor Moffat.

Night had fallen, and our dog was nowhere to be found. There was only one thing to do: drive back to Utah and hope to find the Ranch Exit where we had stopped earlier. I got dressed while Bonnie filled a dish with water for Moffat, just in case I was lucky enough to find her. It must have been around 10 p.m. when I headed back to Utah. I was stunned by the situation. I felt terrible and tried to remember where that Ranch Exit could have been. Was it 100 miles, 75 miles, or 50 miles from home? I thought it was at least 50 miles. In the darkness, I watched the odometer closely while keeping an eye on the exit signs, trying to estimate where we might have left Moffat. I saw the first Ranch Exit at 35 miles, but it had to be further. I continued heading west into the night. Then I saw another Ranch Exit, but it just didn’t feel right. When I reached fifty miles, I decided to take the next exit. As that exit came into view, I was determined to try it. As I slowed to approach the exit, I realized we had left Moffat on the south side of I-70 while heading east. I would have to exit and take the overpass to reach the area where we might have left Moffat six hours earlier.

As I gradually approached the exit ramp, I rolled down the window and started calling out. As I drove toward the overpass ramp, I wondered if it was the right exit or if it was ten miles further west. How could this have happened—poor, sweet Moffat? Suddenly, I heard a rattling sound, like the tags on Moffat's collar. Without warning, she dashed out of the darkness toward the bus. I was in shock. She had managed to stay put, waiting for her humans to rescue her and avoiding coyotes. When I reached the exit, she might have been on the other side of I-70. She probably saw or heard the bus and then heard me calling. Wherever she was, she was now heading for the bus door and leaped into my lap, showering me with kisses of joy. I remember the water not staying in the dish on the bus floor—there was too much excitement.

Of course, there were no cell phones in 1977, so I couldn't share the incredible good fortune with Bonnie. After holding Moffat for a while, I went up the exit, crossed over I-70, and headed east. Moffat would not sit anywhere except on my lap, and we were on our way home.

Denver Broncos: My Team

Remember when I met Ollie Matson at age ten and became a fan of the NFL's Chicago Cardinals? Like the Cardinals, who struggled in the late 1950s before being sold and moved to St. Louis—my new team, the Denver Broncos—also struggled to win, finally having a winning season in 1973. They had moments of competitiveness, and in 1977, they won the Western Division, earning a shot at the Super Bowl. They won their first playoff game against the Pittsburgh Steelers and had to beat the hated Oakland Raiders on New Year's Day in the American Football Conference Championship to advance to the Super Bowl.

As a devoted Broncos fan, the 1977 season felt like a dream—only two regular-season losses, one to Oakland and another to Dallas. I was living in Grand Junction, watching every game and even drinking Orange Crush, the nickname for the Broncos' defense. I couldn't wait to see that game in my living room. But then something incredible happened—Rick Schwartz, a college roommate, called on Friday, December 30. "Jerry, I have two tickets for the game on Sunday, but I doubt you would want to drive 250 miles on icy roads to get to Denver." Icy roads wouldn't be a problem. I said absolutely. He invited Bonnie and me to stay with him and Helene, another college friend, and go to Mile High Stadium on Sunday.

New Year's Day in Denver was clear and cold, with temperatures around ten degrees. Rick and I put on our warmest clothes and headed to the stadium. We arrived early and sat in the west stands, where we enjoyed some sun for a while. It was pretty cold just sitting there, but by kickoff, the temperature was near twenty degrees, and our focus was entirely on the game. The cold made it a tough day; Denver missed three field goals and an extra point. With three minutes left, the Raiders scored to cut the Broncos' lead to 20-17. It was tense. The Broncos had the ball, but with the cold, fumbles were a possibility. If Kenny Stabler of the Raiders got the ball back, we could lose. The Broncos ran out the clock, securing their spot in the Super Bowl against the Dallas Cowboys. That didn't go well, as Denver lost 27-10, marking their first of eight Super Bowl appearances, during which they won three championships. But it was a fantastic season, and it was my first playoff game—the second would be in 1983 with Trish and the Chicago White Sox.

Thank you, Rick! An unforgettable memory.

Chapter 10: Opportunity Knocks

Harvard Bound

In the summer of 1978, while still working in Grand Junction, I was invited to participate in the Employment and Training Institute at Harvard University's John F. Kennedy School of Government. Bonnie, Jenny, and I drove our VW camper van to Libertyville to pick up my mother, who then joined us for the trip to Boston. The VW bus often broke down, so I was always relieved to be closer to Boston at the end of each day. I didn't want to miss the program's orientation and the first day of classes. We rented a garden apartment at 322 Beacon Street in Boston. Each morning, I took the Massachusetts Bay Transportation Authority (MBTA) bus across the Charles River to the Harvard campus in Cambridge. On weekends, we explored as tourists, visiting Cape Cod, Nantucket, and Sturbridge Village, walking the Freedom Trail in Boston, riding the Swan Boats in Boston Common, and traveling up the Maine coast. Although the state did not cover expenses, I received my regular salary. Attending classes with distinguished economists, CETA directors, and staff from across the nation was an incredible learning opportunity.

Turning the Program Around

In late fall of 1978, I had lunch with Bob Ore, the Executive Director of the Colorado Department of Labor and Employment. Bob was a member of the Governor's cabinet. It was a friendly conversation, and he was curious about my experiences and the knowledge I had gained at Harvard. I rambled about my newfound insights and shared a few ideas for improving the administration of the Colorado Balance of State CETA (BOS/CETA) program. The BOS/CETA was responsible for delivering services in 54 rural counties. Bob expressed concern about the poor management at the central office. The following week, I received a call from him, inviting me to spend six weeks in Denver to help address operational issues at the central office of the Colorado BOS/CETA program. Given the significant administrative challenges, what started as a short-term role quickly became a full-time position. At 32, I lacked formal management education or training and was learning as I went. After five months of commuting and with my appointment as director still not official, we became homeowners again, purchasing our fifth house in Arvada.

The enormous task Bob gave me was to revive a program that had been pushed aside to the Division of Employment and Training, which mainly handled the state's Unemployment Insurance System and the Job Service. These were important state programs, but BOS/CETA was seen as an afterthought. To make matters worse, the neglected BOS/CETA office was in disarray.

Bob asked me to assess the situation and make improvements. The first step was to relocate the program to the Office of the Executive Director. I traveled from Grand Junction to Denver nearly every week, with the state covering my travel and lodging costs. I stayed at the Colburn Hotel (now listed on the National Register of Historic Places — it was historic when I stayed there forty-seven years ago), just two blocks from the office, which allowed me to start early and work late. Bob dismissed the director and appointed me as the acting director. The role was demanding, but the staff felt more motivated and received increased attention from the Executive Director. They responded positively to the changes I proposed.

The acting director position was a temporary appointment that lasted much longer than expected. For over a year, I received the salary from my previous position rather than the pay for the role I was actually performing, with no guarantee of a permanent assignment. My short-term appointments in Pueblo and Grand Junction were each finalized within six months. My frustration led me to apply for the same job in Montana. They flew me there for an oral exam, where I tied for first place with Gary Curtis, who was also temporarily acting in a similar capacity in Montana. After being considered for the Montana position, my Colorado job was suddenly posted, and I was then certified. A free trip to Helena, Montana, prompted the state of Colorado to take some action on my long-awaited appointment. And Gary received the Montana job I didn't want.

Colorado State Capitol

After eighteen months, Bob Ore added the evaluation below to my file. The program experienced a remarkable turnaround. A note to that effect from Governor Lamm is included later in this chapter.

> *This evaluation encompasses a period during which the employee served as a Special Assistant to the Executive Director. In the period of this evaluation and under all factors, a special note of thanks and recognition is warranted. Jerry assisted the Executive Director and Deputy Director in effectuating a transition in program design and management that required extra time and professionalism, without which none of the accomplishments would have been possible. Jerry's dedication and work are primarily responsible for improving not only the quality of the programs and the morale of the staff, but also the public image and value of the CETA programs, and are hereby recognized accordingly.*

A New Title

My new title was Director of Colorado's Office of Rural Job Training. My office managed $23 million (projected to be valued at $118 million in 2025) for work and training initiatives across 54 rural counties, including programs for seasonal migrant farmworkers. Additionally, I oversaw programs for the Southern Ute and Ute Mountain Ute Tribes, two of the three federally recognized entities of the Ute Nation. I worked closely with Tribal Chairman Leonard Birch of the Southern Utes and Scott Yellowjacket from the Ute Mountain Utes. Scott Yellowjacket was so upset with my predecessor that he did not want him back on the reservation, so Chairman Yellowjacket told him, "I never want you to cross the cattle guard again." Through effective communication and responsiveness, I fostered constructive, mutually beneficial relationships with both Tribes.

When I hired Arnold Ahkeah, a Navajo Tribal member, to work at the Ute Mountain Ute reservation, I was unaware of the longstanding, intense rivalry between the Navajo and Ute people. I wondered if I had made a poorly informed decision. However, after assigning Arnold to the role, I quickly realized he was the right fit. We had previously faced attendance issues at training sessions and job sites on the reservation. Despite his modesty, Arnold was outstanding. He refused to accept a "no," and with his positive attitude and determination, he helped the program succeed during his time on the reservation.

We held monthly meetings in Denver with the three area administrators. Merlin Smith, who managed the southern area in Pueblo, had previously replaced me in the CETA role there in 1975. He was a veteran of the Army, serving in World War II, the Korean War, and the Vietnam War, starting as a private and retiring as a major. Merlin was always very serious and often fondly recalled his Army days, especially his experiences in Vietnam, where he had the demanding task of briefing General Westmoreland, the Commander of U.S. Forces in Vietnam, each morning. During our meetings, when Merlin was briefing me, he would become stressed and inadvertently refer to the Southern Area office as the Southern Area Command. We all appreciated his service and earnestness; however, I did not resemble General Westmoreland.

Helping at the Statehouse

I was fortunate to work with Governor Dick Lamm and Lt. Governor Nancy Dick on many occasions. I often supported the Lieutenant Governor during her *"Capital for a Day"* campaign across the state, which aimed to make the Lamm/Dick administration more accessible to the public. As a token of appreciation, I received invitations to events at the governor's mansion, which was always exciting.

I had the honor of representing Governor Lamm and delivering a speech at the Ludlow Massacre Memorial Service organized by the United Mine Workers of America (UMWA). An additional speaker was one of the few surviving witnesses of the massacre. This annual event, held since 1916, honors the site in southern Colorado where coal miners went on strike in 1914. The Massacre, which took place on April 20, 1914, was a pivotal moment in the Colorado Coalfield War of 1913-14. On that day, soldiers from the Colorado National Guard and private guards hired by the Colorado Fuel and Iron Company (CF&I) attacked a tent colony of about 1,200 striking coal miners and their families in Ludlow, Colorado. At least twenty-one people, mostly miners' wives and children, lost their lives.

Vote for the Kid from the Dusty Road

In March 1980, Governor Lamm appointed me to the Employment and Training Subcommittee of the Human Resources Committee of the National Governors Association (NGA). This was exciting. When I attended the first meeting, I realized the group's agenda would not directly help me make BOS/CETA an effective program. My job was to provide effective services across a 54-county area, and I had a lot to learn. This subcommittee was not focused on delivering services at the local level, which was my primary responsibility.

Primarily serving rural counties, I was drawn to the Rural Job Training Committee of the National Association of Counties (NACo) to learn from CETA directors across rural America. I attended a committee meeting and the Employment and Training Conference in July 1979. Although being appointed by the Governor to the NGA subcommittee was an honor, the NACo organization offered more opportunities to connect with other job-training professionals. My involvement greatly benefited the BOS/CETA program, allowing me to network with directors nationwide.

I was very active in our six-state Rocky Mountain region, which led my fellow CETA directors to nominate me to the board of NACo's affiliate, the National Association of County Employment and Training Administrators (NACETA). When I attended my first board meeting in Seattle in September 1980, some board members were uneasy about my presence because of my role as a state director and not working for a county. They wanted a formal election process. I returned to Denver, determined to prove my value. Ballots were sent to all CETA directors in the region, and I was elected. In November, at the conference in San Antonio, Bexar County, Texas, I officially joined the board. Later, Colorado's Eagle County commissioners appointed me as their NACo delegate, changing my status. I was no longer just a state director.

After just one year on the board, I ran for NACETA vice president alongside Judy Ann Miller, the CETA director from Contra Costa County, California. She was the current vice president, and her nomination by President Reagan as Assistant Secretary of Defense changed the course of events. Judy and I had teamed up, and, unexpectedly, with her departure, I was suddenly the candidate for NACETA president, with the election less than two months away.

I was elected president in December 1981 in New Orleans, Louisiana, an event that greatly influenced my future work with NACo. After the election, I served as the moderator for a plenary session attended by 1,200 people. The keynote speaker was US Senator Howard Metzenbaum from Ohio. Since the election had happened the day before, there were many "Jerry McNeil for President" signs and stickers around. When the senator began his speech, he congratulated me on my victory. He said he wasn't surprised by the outcome, pointing out the signs all over the hotel, even in the men's room, and the stickers on the glasses at the earlier reception. He joked that he wanted my team to run his next election campaign.

In just over three years, I experienced significant career growth. I went from being a Western Area Administrator in Grand Junction to attending Harvard's John F. Kennedy School of Government. Later, the Executive Director of the Colorado Department of Labor and Employment entrusted me with transforming the BOS/CETA program, which was in disarray. Eventually, I was elected president of a national organization dedicated to employment and training. It was truly an exhilarating period!

A Note from Governor Lamm

In December 1982, the US Department of Labor recognized the Colorado BOS/CETA program for having the highest job placement rates for both adults and youth in the six-state Rocky Mountain area. This achievement ranked the program among the nation's best. The Governor praised the BOS/CETA team, and I shared in that pride as well.

U.S. Department of Labor

Employment and Training Administration
1961 Stout Street
Denver, Colorado 80294

December 9, 1982

8TGC

Honorable Richard D. Lamm
Governor of Colorado
State Capitol Building, Room 136
Denver, Colorado 80203

Dear Governor Lamm:

Based upon an analysis of key performance data for the year ending September 30, 1982, Colorado's "Balance of State" Comprehensive Employment and Training Act (CETA) Program achieved the highest level of putting people in jobs of all such programs in the Region VIII six State area.

I wish to congratulate you, your Director, Jerry McNeil, and the staff working in the Colorado Balance of State CETA System, for the excellent job that was done in providing employment and training services to the unemployed residents in the 54 Counties making up this service delivery area. The programs serving adults achieved better than a 71% entered employment rate and those programs serving youth achieved a 93% positive termination rate. Not only does this place Colorado first among the 21 prime sponsors in Region VIII but also places you near the top nationally.

Best wishes for continued success in meeting the needs of Colorado's employers and unemployed residents.

Sincerely,

Luis Sepúlveda

LUIS SEPULVEDA
Regional Administrator

Jerry –
Good work – I'm proud
of you + your people.
Please extend my thanks

1982, Governor Lamm expressed pride in our team

STATE OF COLORADO

EXECUTIVE CHAMBERS
136 State Capitol
Denver, Colorado 80203
Phone (303) 866-2471

Richard D. Lamm,
Governor

December 24, 1981

Jerald T. McNeil
Director
Balance-of-State/CETA
Colorado Department of
Employment and Labor
1200 Lincoln Street
Denver, CO 80203

Dear Jerry:

Congratulations! I was pleased to hear that your bid for the National Association of County Employment and Training Administrator's Presidency was successful. Your efforts to improve this country's employment and training system have been recognized by your colleagues.

Your election places you in an important leadership position as new employment and training legislation is considered. It has become increasingly evident that the federal government has a role and a responsibility in the improved utilization of our human resources. Your work will help define that federal role as well as the role of State and local governments.

I wish you success during the difficult year ahead. I know you will represent the interests of poor and unemployed Americans and the people of Colorado.

Sincerely,

Richard D. Lamm
Governor

1981, Governor Lamm's congratulations on my election

COLORADO AFL-CIO

300 DENVER LABOR CENTER • 360 ACOMA STREET • DENVER, COLORADO 80223 • PHONE 303/733-2401

PRESIDENT
Norman N. Pledger

SECRETARY-TREASURER
Zelda Bronsted

ASST. TO THE PRESIDENT
Tim G. Flores

COPE-VIP DIRECTOR
Kathy Oatis

VICE PRESIDENTS
Frederick Dean Ames
Billy J. Austin
Kathy Bacino
Carl R. Baer
James Blair
Louise S. Byrnes
Donald J. DeMent
Richard C. Eckenroth
Paul Embrick
Max L. Flint
Don Fortunato
Joe Ganova
Tasso Harris
Gilbert Herrera
Robert Knapp
Ellen C. Lavroff
John A. Maroney
Charles E. Mercer
Ralph E. Miller
Ron Moeder
Lawrence D. Narey
Robert G. Pierson
Robbie Robinson
Ben R. Rountree
Tracy J. Smith
Frank D. Touze
Ray R. Valdez
Karen Vannoy
Paul R. Wilson

November 24, 1982

The Honorable Richard D. Lamm
Governor, State of Colorado
136 State Capitol Building
Denver, Co. 80203

Dear Governor Lamm:

I would like to take this opportunity to extend my personal thanks to you for the fine job that your administrator, Jerry McNeil has done in behalf of the Balance of State, (CETA) for the past few years.

Mr. McNeil has given me excellent cooperation, and has demonstrated deep concern and compassion toward the disadvantaged population in Colorado.

I feel it would be very beneficial to the disadvantaged citizens of Colorado to continue the fine work of the Balance of State office as the administrators of the Joint Training Parntership Act, Service Delivery Area for Colorado.

Again, I would like to commend Mr. McNeil and his staff for the work they have done in the past and I sincerely hope that you will consider this recommendation when making your decision for the future.

With my kindest personal regards, I remain

Norm

Norman N. Pledger, President
Colorado AFL-CIO

NNP/b

cc: Roy Romer
David Miller

1982, A letter from the President of the Colorado AFL-CIO to Governor Lamm.

STATE OF COLORADO

EXECUTIVE CHAMBERS
136 State Capitol
Denver, Colorado 80203
Phone (303) 866-2471

Richard D. Lamm
Governor

December 13, 1982

Mr. Jerald T. McNeil
CETA Balance of State
Department of Labor and Employment
1200 Lincoln Street, Room 620
Denver, Colorado 80203

Dear Jerry:

I was very pleased to receive the enclosed letter from Norman Pledger commending you for your excellent, concerned and compassionate performance on behalf of the CETA Balance of State.

I would like to take this opportunity to add my thanks to Norm's. Your fine performance not only reflects highly on you but also on the State of Colorado and its employees.

Thanks again for your dedication to your job.

Sincerely,

Richard D. Lamm
Governor

Enclosure

cc: Ruben Valdez, Executive Director
Department of Labor and Employment

John Kezer, Director
Division of Employment and Training

1982, "...Reflects highly on you, but also the State of Colorado", Governor Lamm

1980, With Colorado Congresswoman
Pat Schroeder, in Washington, D.C.

1981, Running for National President,
representing Eagle County

County News

Official Publication of The National Association of Counties

Block grants alter state, local roles

As states begin to implement the health and human services block grants, new attention is being focused on the relationship between state and local governments. This week, the "New Federalism Report" looks at the issues and outlines actions taken by a number of states. Page 3

Federalism plan unites localities

The leaders of state and local governments across the country are coming together to oppose administration plans that threaten to take an even larger bite out of federal grants to them. The disenchantment began when localities took the lion's share of the first round of budget cuts and then discovered that still more cuts were at hand. Neal Peirce comments on the problems. Page 4

METZENBAUM

Congress to vote on new spending cut

During Employment Policy Conference

Officials vow to fight to fund CETA

NEW ORLEANS, La.—More than 1,000 of the nation's leading elected county officials and professional employment directors met here last week and heard J. Richard Conder, president of the National Association of Counties (NACo), and other top government executives urge Congress to fund job training under the CETA program at the $3.6 billion level, and not at lesser levels proposed by the Reagan administration.

Conder told delegates to the 10th National Employment Policy Conference that the nation, with a current 8.4 percent unemployment rate, cannot afford to reduce special training for the young, disadvantaged, or those put out of work due to changes in technology.

"America's counties are dedicated to ensuring that every man, woman and child in our nation has an opportunity to obtain the education and training necessary to enter the work force as part of our great economic system," said American dream to every person in our society. We must continue to fund the Comprehensive Employment and Training Act (CETA) program at current levels."

Delegates from the National Association of County Employment and Training Administrators (NACETA), the NACo affiliate which sponsored the conference, also elected a new slate of officers. Jerald McNeil, balance-of-state representative for CETA in Colorado, is the new president, and Tim Smith, CETA director, Montgomery County, Ohio, is the new vice president. Robert N. "Skip" Johnston, CETA director, Broward County, Fla., was elected to be NACETA's representative to the NACo board.

Delegates also took a tough stand on federal employment programs. The Employment Steering Committee approved a resolution urging Congress and the Reagan administration to recognize and continue the explicit leadership

McNEIL

Employment and Training Act.

The steering committee also opposed any further cuts in the CETA programs. A resolution approved by the committee opposes the CETA funding levels for fiscal 1983 proposed by the Office of Management and Budget

1981, After the Election

Chapter 11: Tri-State Consortium for Energy Training

Oil Shale Boom

Following the 1973 OPEC oil embargo, adapting to changing circumstances became essential. Conservation, efficiency, and alternative energy sources were vital. My work with CETA in southeastern and western Colorado focused on developing synthetic fuels and alternative energy sources, including solar energy and coal gasification, while also supporting the state's coal mining industry.

The CETA program supported the development of ethanol (ethyl alcohol) in southeastern Colorado. Ethanol was made from corn and mixed with gasoline at a 10:90 ratio, known as gasohol. This process was also crucial for corn producers in the area.

Our efforts also included training in passive solar techniques. We established and implemented training programs in various counties across the state. Through CETA's Public Service Employment, this initiative installed passive solar systems in rural homes. Colorado Governor Dick Lamm narrated a training film we produced on passive solar energy education and implementation, which was presented to high schools throughout the state.

In the 1970s, Tenneco Oil and Shell Corporation collaborated on research to extract oil from shale. Over $200 million was invested in this effort, and the process was seen as commercially viable. In a 1980 white paper on oil shale, Exxon projected a $500 billion investment in what they called "synthetic fuels." This plan involved building 150 oil shale plants over 20 to 30 years and, in the most extreme scenario, establishing six large strip mines. Andrew Gulliford later highlighted this proposal in his 1989 book, "Boomtown Blues." Exxon estimated that each mine would require 22,000 workers and each plant would require 8,000 workers to produce eight million barrels of oil per day by 2010.

While the rest of the country struggled with the energy crisis, Western Colorado experienced unprecedented growth. Tosco, Cleveland-Cliffs, and Standard Oil of Ohio formed a joint venture to develop the

Colony Oil Shale Project, located just north of Parachute, 45 miles east of Grand Junction. As the oil crisis worsened, more organizations joined, including Atlantic Richfield Oil, Ashland Oil, and Occidental Oil Shale. The boom was in full swing. People from all over the country flocked to western Colorado. At a time when regions like the industrial Midwest faced challenges, local blue-collar jobs were plentiful.

Having worked in western Colorado, I recognized the upcoming growth in Colorado, Utah, and Wyoming. Dave Courtney, the manager of Industrial Relations for Occidental Oil Shale, Inc., chaired the Western Area Advisory CETA Council while I was in Grand Junction. My office had strong ties to oil shale projects. Interestingly, in 1978, Dave Courtney invited me to join him at Occidental Oil Shale. There was some misinformation, and Jim Foxx, the Human Resources Manager, thought that since I attended Harvard during the summer, I was not interested; however, I had been interested, but being asked to lead a state agency later in 1978 cooled my enthusiasm.

In 1980, when I was the director of Colorado's Balance of State CETA program, twelve counties on the western slope had significant energy resources.

Volcanic ash covered my car as I drove to Stapleton Airport in Denver for my first visit to the nation's capital. It was May 19, 1980, just a day after the eruption of Mt. St. Helens. I attended a conference hosted by the US Department of Energy at the Shoreham Hotel in Washington, D.C., which focused on workforce challenges in energy-related sectors. While sitting in the audience during a plenary session, I reflected on the difficulties of training the thousands of workers needed for oil shale development. Effectively managing the essential workforce—including miners, welders, chemical lab specialists, transportation workers, construction workers, and mechanics—was crucial to preventing costly, time-consuming delays. There might be a way to meet this demand. If Colorado, Utah, and Wyoming collaborated, they could reduce duplication of training programs, share resources, and address issues related to state boundaries.

A Tri-State Consortium for Energy Training could solve the issue. Is this feasible? What steps are needed to set it up? Who would manage the consortium? During my flights from DC to Chicago and Denver, I thought about the opportunities and planned a strategy to move forward.

To thoroughly evaluate this proposal, I consulted with the director of the state's CETA Special Grants Office and discussed it with my program staff. I also met with Bob Orr, who responded positively. As a member of Gov. Lamm's cabinet, he presented the idea to the Governor. This process moved quickly. I explained the concept to the job-training directors in Utah and Wyoming.

At the Rocky Mountain Six-State Region CETA directors' meeting in Helena, Montana, I arranged a meeting with the directors from Utah and Wyoming. We discussed the idea of a Tri-State Consortium, which had sparked interest during our initial phone conversations. Each state was already preparing for the impacts of synthetic fuel development. We reached an agreement on several key goals.

- Eliminate redundant training programs,
- Distribute training resources according to labor needs.
- Reduce or eliminate out-of-state tuition fees.

After the Helena meeting, we quickly drafted a consortium agreement and collaborated closely with each state's Occupational Coordinating Committee (OCC). We used econometric modeling to project future labor needs for synthetic fuel development, highlighting the importance of the Tri-State Energy Training Consortium.

My two colleagues, Allan Ayab from Utah and Frank Galleotos from Wyoming, worked on the same projects for their respective states. When fall arrived, Utah quickly committed, but Wyoming hesitated.

This required a trip to Laramie, Wyoming, for a meeting. I was accompanied by Bob Orr and Monte Pascoe, Colorado's Executive Director for Natural Resources. We flew in a single-engine state plane piloted by a Colorado State Patrol officer. The flight was quite cozy. I sat next to the pilot, while Bob and Monte sat beside each other just behind me.

Although Cheyenne is the state capital, Wyoming Governor Edgar Herschler's staff chose to hold the meeting at the University of Wyoming in Laramie. The Wyoming cabinet members had only a 49-mile drive, which allowed economics and natural resources professors at the university to attend and later provide recommendations to the governor and his key staff.

We arrived in Laramie in the afternoon, and the meeting lasted for several hours. Many insightful questions and suggestions came up about how the consortium could operate more effectively. The last hour shifted from promoting the consortium idea to Wyoming to making it beneficial for all three states. It ended on a positive note.

After leaving the university, a cold wind announced the arrival of a Rocky Mountain fall storm. On our way to the airport, we all felt a sense of achievement. The Tri-State consortium was about to be officially launched!

To finalize the agreement, I needed the signatures of three governors: Wyoming's Governor Herschler, Utah's Governor Matheson, and Colorado's Governor Lamm. Governor Lamm was the consortium's lead representative, while I served as the administrator. As I stepped into the Governor's office to get his signature, I was transported back to my first visit to the Capitol when I was just ten years old. It had been a long journey from the two-room school on the Dusty Road in Illinois to the Governor's Office in Colorado.

We began discussions with the US Department of Energy before the agreement was approved, and their staff expressed interest in the idea. After the three governors signed the agreement in the fall of 1980, we submitted the grant proposal to several federal agencies.

The US Navy's Office of Naval Petroleum and Oil Shale Reserves conducted an experimental oil shale project at Anvil Points, Colorado, which extracted 100,000 barrels of shale oil in the late 1970s. The inactive mine site sparked discussions about its potential for training and development. We visited Anvil Points to assess possible applications and the legality of contracting with the consortium.

The consortium quickly secured a grant from the US Navy to fund additional econometric modeling. Once again, we depended on the economist from the Occupation Coordinating Committee in each state.

The Department of Energy grant was awarded through the BDM Corporation. We had a meeting in Washington to review our progress. Surprisingly, Jack Swiegart, their Vice President, chaired the meeting. You might remember him as a crew member on Apollo Thirteen, whose oxygen tank exploded in the Service Module, damaging the spacecraft and forcing the crew to abandon the third lunar landing. It was fascinating to hear him talk about those desperate hours in the Service Module. He definitely knew how to handle a challenging situation. Oil shale would be straightforward.

In the summer of 1981, we hosted a conference in Park City, Utah, attended by educators, industry representatives, local officials, economists, and other stakeholders. This event served as a platform for connecting key individuals from the three states. It offered an opportunity to raise awareness of the consortium and establish a framework for assessing workforce needs in each state, evaluating current capacity to meet immediate demand, and planning for major future initiatives. We compiled an inventory of existing training programs at community colleges, secondary schools, and post-secondary vocational schools. A committee was formed to coordinate the distribution of training resources. As we gained a clearer understanding of our existing training capacity, we began projecting future budget needs in each state. Our work was gaining momentum.

On Sunday, May 2, 1982, a day known locally as Black Sunday, Exxon, the largest oil share investor, announced it was ending its $5 billion investment in the Colony Oil Shale Project, effective immediately. The news hit the Western Slope hard. This sudden decision caused an immediate $85 million loss in annual payroll. Unemployment soared, many banks closed, and businesses shut down permanently. The economic turmoil's aftereffects continued to ripple for years. By February of the following year, Mesa County's unemployment rate peaked at 15.7 percent, while Garfield County's reached 15.2 percent. (The Daily Sentinel, May 4, 1983).

Several factors led to the sudden shutdown of the synthetic fuels initiatives, including falling oil prices, a global recession, and a shift in Exxon's priorities. According to the Denver Post, the decision to stop development of synthetic fuels "was largely driven by a focus on company profit rather than national security."

The Tri-State Consortium for Energy Training's work came to an abrupt end.

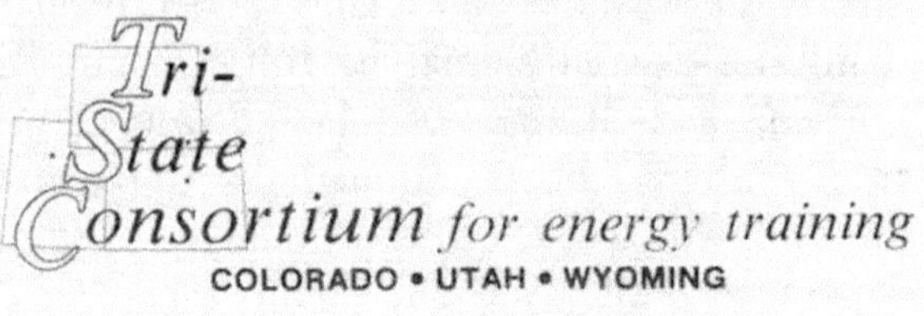

Richard D. Lamm, Governor
COLORADO

Scott M. Matheson, Governor
UTAH

Ed Herschler, Governor
WYOMING

From 1980 to 1982, I served as the administrator of the Tri-State Consortium.

Chapter 12: A Move to the Nation's Capital

Trish Hogue

Trish and I have been happily married for over four decades, and our bond remains unbreakable. From the very beginning, we've been life partners, facing every challenge side by side. While I've always been drawn to the mountains, Trish has always loved the ocean and beaches. We've managed to incorporate both into our lives, sharing our joys and sorrows. Trish has been my unwavering rock, my soulmate, and the love of my life.

When we married, Trish was the Executive Director of the National Commission for Employment Policy. She later became the Administrator of Strategic Planning and Policy Development at the US Department of Labor's Employment and Training Administration. Afterward, she transitioned to private consulting before serving as the Deputy Assistant Secretary for the Office of Adult and Vocational Education at the US Department of Education. President Clinton nominated her to be the Assistant Secretary for the same office, and the US Senate confirmed her.

Since I was also involved in the employment and training field, I was able to join Trish and participate in several international trips to Perth, Western Australia; Aberdeen, Scotland; London, and Paris. In the States, we were often speakers at the same conferences. Now, many years have passed, but we still reminisce about the many people we worked with and knew.

Great American Pastimes Company

In 1984, Trish and I started The Great American Pastimes Company (GAPCo). As a producer, I created a baseball video series, "*Baseball in the News: Classic Movie Theater Newsreels*," and managed a sports video catalog.

We were underfunded; it was an in-house operation. My cousin, Kathy (McNeil) Sherman, designed our logo and cover. Usually, we

PAGE 11

COVER ST

Researcher Reels In The Sports Years

By Martie Zad
Washington Post Staff Writer

Jerald T. McNeil is the director of training and employment programs for the National Association of Counties here in Washington. A few years ago he was collecting material on work and training programs during the depression.

He researched hundreds of newsreels of the 1930s in the National Archives vaults. While compiling the material he was searching for, he found something he wasn't looking for: extensive footage of historic sports events. He was fascinated.

"I found myself spending more time looking at the sports footage than at the stuff I was trying to collect," said McNeil.

He decided to go back and copy enough old baseball film to produce a sports video cassette. What he wound up with was a three-volume set of about 60 minutes each from selected movie theater newsreels with the original sound and narration. He engaged Eemmy-winning film editor Bill Snider of New York and 18 months after he began he had series called, "Baseball in the News" out in the marketplace.

NBC's Tony Kubek endorsed the sereies with: "Every nostalgia buff and purist should have Jerry McNeil's video cassettes of '50s and '60s baseball highlightss. This is REAL baseball, without the DH."

Detroit manager Sparky Anderson said: " 'Baseball in the News' makes me feel young again—great memories."

Hall of Famer Pee Wee Reese said: " 'Baseball In The News' is something fans will want to watch again and again! Seeing Ebbets Field is like going home again."

Jerald T. McNeil displays the sports video volumes he has produced.

Volume one covers events from 1951-55; volume two, 1956-60; and volume three, 1961-67. The cost is $39.95 per volume or $109.95 for the set. Write to: The Great American Pastimes Co., 304 Rucker Place, Alexandria, Va. 22301. McNeil is also marketing a movie he uncovered in The Library of Congress, "The Jackie Robinson Story," in conjunction with Jackie's widow, Rachael, and The Robinson Foundation.

Some of the events McNeil re-captured in his "Baseball In The News" series include: Bobby Thomson's playoff homer for the Miracle Giants of 1951; Joe DiMaggio's last home run in 1951, Ted Williams' return from Korea, the Brooklyn Dodgers finally winning a World Series in 1955, Don Larsen's perfect game in the 1956 World Series, Willie Mays belting four home runs in a game against Milwaukee in 1961, Roger Maris' 61st homer on the final day of the 1961 season, the 1963 New York Mets playing the last baseball game in the Polo Grounds, the Baltimore Orioles sweeping the L.A. Dodgers in the 1967 World Series, and on and on.

There could have been lots more, the 40-year-old McNeil said. "But we only used the film of good quality and sound. Some of the closeups and spring training shots of the great old legends are priceless. My favorites."

August 24, 1986, Washington Post Magazine,

ordered 500 VHS tapes for duplication. Afterward, we labeled each tape, inserted printed covers in plastic cases, and they were ready for sale.

We managed marketing, production, and order fulfillment. With Bill Gilbert's assistance, we launched a promotional campaign. Bill, a well-connected former local newspaperman and author, helped GAPCo gain recognition in both national and regional outlets, including Sports Illustrated, Sporting News, Good Morning America, the *Washington Post*, *Panorama* (a live talk show in Washington, DC), and various trade magazines. He had recently co-written an autobiography with Duke Snider titled *'The Duke of Flatbush.'* Duke was a home-run-hitting center fielder for the Brooklyn Dodgers and a member of the Baseball Hall of Fame. Bill invited Trish and me to the book launch, where we had the chance to visit with the Duke. I still have the book he autographed.

Our main sales outlets for our video included the Smithsonian History Museum gift shop and its catalog. Working on this project rekindled my passion for baseball and gave me the chance to meet many legends and Hall of Fame players. Here are some stories from that time.

It all started when I was researching video and film materials on the Public Works Administration programs of the 1930s at the National Archives, where I discovered the Universal Studios Movie Theater News Reels. Home video players were introduced in the late 1970s and quickly gained popularity. Because of my love for baseball, I was captivated by footage from the 1930s through 1967. I soon shifted my focus from work programs to baseball history. I took the subway from Alexandria with my rented Sony 3/4-inch U-Matic VCR, which weighed over 30 pounds. I spent weeks recording all the newsreels on baseball and related personalities.

While working at the Archives, I considered how best to prepare the material for sale. My ideas were similar to those introduced by Ken Burns several years earlier, but I lacked the experience and resources to approach a project in that way.

Since some early-year material lacked audio, I concentrated on newsreels from 1951 to 1967, which preserved their original sound and narration. As I had no experience with video editing, I had to hire someone. Consequently, I spent weeks reviewing the footage and meticulously noting the elements I desired in the final product. The footage I selected spanned approximately three hours, so I divided it into three separate videos.

Before I proceeded, I needed to verify whether using the newsreels was legal. Trish and I hired Ben Zelenko and his firm. Ben was counsel for the American Society of Composers, Authors, and Publishers (ASCAP) and the National Football Players Association, and he was a former counsel to the US House of Representatives Committee on the Judiciary. Ben knew his way around the legalities and was familiar with the executives at Universal Studios. He assured us the material was in the public domain, but he also contacted Universal Studios to confirm our project didn't violate any laws.

At that point, we teamed up with Bill Snider from Boulder, Colorado, to edit the content, film the introductions, closings, and interludes. I had previously worked on a project with Bill in Colorado; he was an award-winning editor and cinematographer. Bill and I traveled to the Babe Ruth Birthplace Museum in Baltimore to film baseball memorabilia for the intros and endings. We had full access to everything in the museum. I even got to swing the bat of Home Run Baker, the home run king before Babe Ruth. With the videos in production, I shifted my focus to promotion.

In the spring of 1984, I met Chuck Stevens in his office in Garden Grove, California. He served as the Secretary of the Professional Baseball Players Association of America, an organization that united former baseball players, coaches, and umpires to assist those in need. Chuck was enthusiastic about the video project and generously provided a letter of introduction and support for me to use when reaching out to former major league players.

Talking with Chuck was one of the highlights of the video project. He shared many stories from his time in baseball. Chuck played for the St. Louis Browns in the 1940s, but his career was interrupted by World War II. After his major league career, he spent six years playing in the Pacific Coast League.

Chuck appeared in the 1949 sports film *"The Stratton Story,"* starring Jimmy Stewart as Monty Stratton and June Allyson as his wife, Ethel. He also appeared in *"The Winning Team"* (1952), featuring Ronald Reagan as Grover Cleveland Alexander and Doris Day as Aimee Arrants Alexander. We discussed his experiences making movies, and he mentioned that Bob Lemon was also part of *"The Winning Team."* Later that year, I spent time with Bob Lemon and learned more about how he helped Ronald Reagan portray a major league pitcher in the film.

When I spoke to a former player, I always mentioned Chuck Stevens, and no player ever refused to help me. We received all the endorsements thanks to Chuck's support.

It was always an incredible experience to talk with Hall of Fame players. One memorable instance occurred when I had the opportunity to visit with Bob Feller at the Mayflower Hotel before the Old Timers game at RFK Stadium. He was a superstar with the Cleveland Indians and a Hall of Famer since 1962, and was delighted to assist me. However, he did confess that he lacked a VCR. Nevertheless, he expressed his intention to acquire one so that he could watch *"Baseball in the News."*

In 1986, I appeared on a noontime talk show hosted by Maury Povich in Washington, D.C. Maury was especially interested in the videos because his father, Shirley Povich, was a famous sports writer who worked for The Washington Post for 55 years and was inducted into the National Sportswriters Hall of Fame in 1984. As a kid, Maury had been to the spring training locations shown in the video. Unfortunately, he did not appear in the segment. It was incredible to be in the green room with Michelle Phillips from the Mamas and the Papas, Robert

Merrill from the Metropolitan Opera, and Norman Lloyd, a TV and movie actor; they all wanted to discuss "*Baseball in the News*." (At this time, I was in transition, working at NACo and continuing to promote the video series.)

That night, I was supposed to attend a reception at the Hyatt Regency, just a block from my office. I was heading to the Montana Association of Counties Conference in Miles City the next morning and was running out of time. I planned to make a quick appearance before heading home to get ready for an early flight the next day. However, my visit was extended because I met Julie Nixon Eisenhower, Richard Nixon's daughter, who was married to David Eisenhower, the grandson of President Dwight D. Eisenhower. We ended up talking about baseball, and the conversation ran long. She was very interested in *Baseball in the News,* and she knew her husband, David, would be excited to see it. She wrote their Pennsylvania home address on the back of my business card, and I promised to send them the videotape. Running late, I rushed home to prepare for my early flight and planned to send the tape when I returned. However, somewhere between the Hyatt Regency, the apartment in Alexandria, and Miles City, the card with the address was lost. If only I had had an iPhone.

One phone call that I'll never forget was from Ernie Harwell, a legendary baseball announcer who spent 55 years with four teams, including 42 years with the Detroit Tigers. He also called many of NBC Radio's All-Star games and World Series, as well as CBS Radio's Game of the Week. The Hall of Fame recognized his contributions to baseball by awarding him the Ford C. Frick Award. When I answered the phone, he said, "This is Ernie Harwell. Is this Jerry?" His voice was instantly recognizable, and he didn't need to introduce himself; his voice was all I needed to know who he was. He continued, "I saw the article about your videos in Sports Illustrated and would like to send them to a friend in St. Louis. Can I do that now?" We discussed a few segments from the videos and talked about baseball in the 1950s and 1960s. It was an incredible experience. Then I told him he could place an order. I gave him the cost and our address, and since we didn't accept credit cards, he could send a check. I also assured him that I would mail the tapes the next day. I wish I had been able to record that call; I would love to replay it over and over.

Meeting my baseball heroes through the video project was a fantastic experience. We received incredible support from many Hall of Fame members.

Kudos for Baseball in the News

"*Baseball in the News* is something baseball fans will want to watch again and again! It is timeless; as the years go by, it will become even more of a collector's item. Seeing Ebbets Field is like going home again!"

Pee Wee Reese
Brooklyn Dodgers
Baseball Hall of Fame 1984

"*Baseball in the News* makes me feel like a kid again; great memories! This truly captures an outstanding era in the history of our national pastime."

Sparky Anderson
Manager
World Champion Detroit Tigers
Baseball Hall of Fame 2000

"All baseball buffs will be eager to buy *Baseball in the News* and start a collection."

Hank Greenberg
Detroit Tigers
Baseball Hall of Fame 1956

"To put it simply, *Baseball in the News* is a great way to step back to baseball of thirty years ago. The Newsreels tell it like it was. A must-have addition to any baseball collection!

Willie Stargell
Pittsburgh Pirates
Baseball Hall of Fame 1988

"It's terrific! All baseball fans will want to have *Baseball in the News*. I love those baggy pants!"

Lefty Gomez
New York Yankees
Baseball Hall of Fame 1972

"This videotape brings back great memories. It's terrific to see so many Hall of Famers in action. This is baseball nostalgia at its best!"

Bob Feller
Cleveland Indians
Baseball Hall of Fame 1962

"*Baseball in the News* is absolutely a rare and classy production. It's first-rate. It is a terrific part of my video library."

Early Wynn
Cleveland Indians and Chicago White Sox
Baseball Hall of Fame 1972

"*Baseball in the News* is a pitch straight down the middle for baseball buffs."

Sports Illustrated

"*Baseball In The News* takes you back to the grand old days of baseball via live newsreel coverage you may have forgotten existed."

Jack Lang
Executive Secretary of the Baseball Writers' Association of America

In 2025, Baseball in the News remains available on Amazon as a DVD or download.

The Potomac River First Day Club

New Year's Day was a wonderful time with friends and family as we ushered in the new year by the Potomac River. We would go to the Riverside Picnic area along the George Washington Memorial Highway, just north of Mount Vernon. Our menu featured coffee, orange juice, hot chocolate, sausage links, and French toast, all cooked on a charcoal grill brought from home. We kept the coffee and hot water warm using a Coleman camp stove.

At the first club event, Trish, Allison, and I recited poems and enjoyed hot chocolate. The following year, we added family, including Rocky, Trish's brother, and his family. Over the years, my children, mother, and friends joined in, and the game of touch football became a lot of fun. Initially, it was the kids against the parents, but as the kids grew older, the dynamic shifted. We made French toast batter at home and cooked it on-site. Since New Year's Day was often cold, everyone bundled up. We started at ten and finished by one. It was a busy morning with food prep, loading the grill, and packing everything into the car.

The group grew to include over 35 family and friends, from young children to grandparents. It was a wonderful way to connect with loved ones as we entered the new year. It felt especially meaningful for the children. While New Year's Eve is usually for adults, there was now also a time to welcome the new year with family, including mom, dad, kids, grandma, and grandpa. I hope those children have fond memories of New Year's Day on the Potomac River.

When Trish, Dan, and I bought a country house in Winchester, Virginia, that's where we spent the Christmas and New Year's holidays. So, no more First Day Club. However, our friend Beth Buehlmann continued the tradition of gathering at her house for several decades, and a few years ago, we joined via Zoom.

National Association of Counties

In September 1985, I was offered the role of Director of Employment and Training Programs at NACo, mainly because I had served as president of NACETA. Trish and I attended a conference in Perth, Australia, where Trish was the keynote speaker, so I had to delay starting my new position until we returned. On our way back, we visited our friends John Wallace and Ellen Rashbaum in San Francisco. While at their home, I received troubling news over the phone: the manager who hired me had been dismissed.

Once again, I took over a program in the midst of a sharp decline. Membership had decreased, and staffing levels were at their lowest point. The immediate focus was on preparing for the upcoming Employment and Training/Human Services Conference scheduled for November in Atlanta, Fulton County, Georgia. Suddenly, I found myself with a significant responsibility. It felt like a baptism by fire, but in the end, everything went smoothly. The workshops were well attended, and the food was good. Jesse Jackson, a well-known civil rights leader, delivered a powerful speech at the conference.

I survived the conference, expanded my staff, and then focused on outreach with county employment and training directors while improving the quality of our services. As I reflected on this effort, I saw that these steps, building on one another, ultimately resulted in a successful and noteworthy program.

Governor Dukakis

My first conference was a success. The second conference in Broward County, Florida, took place in November 1986, and we had another engaging speaker.

The story begins on June 30, 1986, when Trish and I were in Boston for work and had tickets to see the Red Sox play the Toronto Blue Jays. We were busy all day, and when we returned to the Parker House Hotel to get ready for our trip to Fenway Park, we received a call from our friend Beth Buehlman, who wished us a happy second anniversary. We were shocked to realize we had completely forgotten it was June 30. Thanks for the reminder, Beth.

So, what kept us so busy that day? After several meetings, we headed to the Massachusetts State House for one more meeting. As we entered the gates and approached the State House, we passed the statues of Daniel Webster and Horace Mann.

This was the new statehouse built in 1798, replacing the original statehouse constructed in 1713. It is hard to miss with its gold dome. What an ornate and historic building with stained glass, murals, statuary, and marble floors and walls. It felt like stepping into history. We made our way to the third floor to an office marked "Governor." We were heading into a meeting with Governor Michael Dukakis. First, we entered the Governor's Waiting Room, decorated with portraits of past governors. When we entered his office, the governor was energetic and enthusiastic in his greeting. We were there to learn about the Massachusetts Welfare-to-Work Program, and he had a compelling story to tell.

The office was spacious, facing south with a view across Beacon Street to the Boston Common. A conference table was in the center of the room. The group and the Governor took our seats. Gov. Dukakis was quite animated about the state's project. While listening to him, I couldn't help but scan the room.

What stays in my memory nearly forty years later is the portrait of Samuel Adams on the wall above the marble fireplace behind the governor's desk. I sat there thinking about the building's history and the room. The hour-long meeting flew by. It had been a very informative 60 minutes. But then it was time for Trish and me to rush to the hotel, then to Fenway Park.

The Governor's enthusiasm for this critical program made me think he would be an excellent speaker at NACo's Employment and Training/ Human Services Conference in November. Soon after returning to my office, I sent a thank-you note and extended an invitation to Governor Dukakis, who accepted.

In November, over 1,000 county officials, welfare directors, and job-training professionals gathered in Fort Lauderdale, Broward County, Florida. We hosted an informal reception for the Governor and his wife, Kitty, before the Governor's speech. The speech was a great success. The audience responded enthusiastically to his positive and constructive approach to reducing welfare.

Two journalists from the Boston Globe and Boston Herald attended the event. I was responsible for organizing a press availability after the governor's speech and waited with the journalists in a nearby room. When the governor arrived, only four of us were there. The reporters asked many questions, primarily about whether Dukakis planned to run for President in 1988. The conversation was friendly, though he sidestepped the question. One reporter, skeptically, said, “Governor, many people don’t know who you are.” Dukakis, who had just received applause from a thousand county officials praising his leadership, replied, “Well, I think the people out there know me now.”

Gov. Dukakis announced his presidential bid on March 16, 1987, and secured the Democratic nomination in July 1988; however, he ultimately lost to Vice President George H. W. Bush, who, of course, was a big admirer of *Baseball in the News,* as explained in Chapter 17.

More NACo activity

After five years of managing the Employment and Training programs, I established the Environmental Programs Unit using grants from the Environmental Protection Agency for Radon and Indoor Air initiatives, followed by a coastal watershed grant. One of our first watershed briefings was by a new EPA program administrator for the Leaking Underground Storage Tanks program. He visited NACo and was enthusiastic about his new role. He mentioned that his mother was shocked when he told her he was now in charge of LUST in the nation's capital. That was the last funny person at EPA.

Descriptions of my positions at NACo are included in Chapter 19. Here are some highlights. My role and responsibilities evolved over my fourteen years with the organization. Ultimately, I took charge of all NACo’s projects in the Department of County Services. These efforts led to my promotion to Deputy Director of the Department of County Services.

As deputy director, I oversaw and coordinated activities across five divisions: Community Services, Program Development, Training, Research, and Conferences. I secured grants to fund programs and supported county officials. Most of our external funding came from federal grants. We acted as a crucial link between federal agencies and local authorities, helping implement new laws and regulations that required local action. My goal was to deliver on our commitments consistently. We built a reputation for achieving our objectives. I managed budgeting and strategic planning and tracked progress toward goals. Additionally, I represented our department and the Executive Director at various meetings and conferences.

The JEDI Experience

There have been many unforgettable experiences, and here is another: in 1987, I was in a small meeting room in the Sam Rayburn Building. It was during a conference on Senator Ted Kennedy's Jobs for Employable Dependent Individuals (JEDI) program, which was under discussion in the House of Representatives and the Senate. The bill had passed the Senate. This program aimed to provide financial incentives to states to train and place recipients of Aid to Families with Dependent Children (AFDC). The NACo president, a Harvard graduate and a strong Kennedy supporter, initially supported JEDI when it was introduced. However, during the policy review at NACo, many concerns arose, causing NACo to decide not to support the bill. Trish and I watched the debate between Senator Kennedy and Congressman Gus Hawkins, Chair of the House Education and Labor Committee. I was the only NACo representative in the room, and Senator Kennedy was eager to build on the early support from our president, which made headlines in the County News. He held up a copy of the newspaper and declared there was support from the county governments. Mr. Hawkins knew better and quickly corrected the senator, saying that wasn't the case. I felt uneasy, thinking I might need to step in and clarify NACo's position. I wasn't a lobbyist and wasn't prepared to defend NACo's stance on JEDI. However, Mr. Hawkins quickly ended the discussion, stating that the House would not support the bill. Senator Kennedy and his aides stormed out of the room, and the bill subsequently died. It was a valuable experience to observe two senior congressional officials in action and see how quickly legislation can be halted.

Elizabeth Dole's office

In 1989, a power couple in the nation's capital was Elizabeth and Robert Dole. Bob Dole was a US Senator from Kansas, a future presidential candidate and a former attorney for Russell County, Kansas, who would join us most years at the NACo Legislative Conference at the Washington Hilton. He enjoyed reconnecting with county elected officials. Elizabeth Dole was the Secretary of the US Department of Labor, former Secretary of the US Department of Transportation, and a future senator from North Carolina.

Secretary Dole had a superb office location on the southeast corner of the Francis Perkins building on Constitution Avenue. Once, when I was in her office in the late afternoon, she told me why she thought her office location was so great. "From this window, I can see the capital, and if the flag is flying over the Senate, then I know Bob is still working. When it's down, I know Bob is home making dinner."

Senator Paul Simon's Letters

I have a letter from US Senator Paul Simon of Illinois to my mother. She was very ill in 1989. In his letter, he acknowledges her health struggles and hopes she's improving, adding, "You should be proud of the good work your son Jerry is doing." I hope this brought her a small moment of pride, knowing that her five-year-old son, who once helped place milk cartons on lunch tables, had come a long way from the Dusty Road.

After my mom's passing, Senator Simon wrote to me, "Losing your mother is not easy, but I'm sure she was proud of the contribution you have made. Your service is a great tribute to her."

She deserved a great tribute.

Presidential Inaugurations

Trish and I attended Bill Clinton's first inauguration in 1993. We had tickets to stand on Capitol Hill and watch the notable people walk in and take their seats. We also attended his second inauguration and the inaugural ball, sponsored by a Massachusetts delegation, marking my first black-tie event in Washington. Another tuxedo event in D.C. was a black-tie evening hosted by the Organization of American States (OAS). It was a celebration of the partnership among the 35 South American countries, aimed at promoting cooperation and integration. Great fun, but I guess I am not a tuxedo guy.

Rugged Acres

In 1986, my brother Dan, Trish, and I bought a house on a tree farm in Winchester, Virginia. We called it the "Rugged Acres"; it was two hours west of Alexandria, and we visited almost every weekend. It was an incredible refuge where we could escape the stresses of Washington, D.C., for a few days. We spent many Christmases and summer vacations there with the children, including the first two grandchildren. We also enjoyed Thanksgiving at the farm with Dan, Trish's brother, Rocky, his wife, Anja, and their kids, Peter and Jonathan. The property encompassed over 300 acres of oak and pine trees, two beaver ponds, and a diverse array of wildlife, including wild turkeys, deer, and various birds. The Rugged Acres kept me motivated to keep going. Weekends were busy with cutting down dead trees and splitting them for firewood. The old wood-burning furnace kept the house warm on the cold winter days. We also had electric heat, which kept the house from freezing when we were in Alexandria. We also took long walks on the property and often watched the beavers in the two ponds.

Trish changed jobs several times during the 1980s and 1990s. After I started with NACo in 1985, I continued to take on additional responsibilities. Trish was there to support me through it. There were Saturday mornings at the Rugged Acres that felt like we were a thousand miles from work pressures. Winters were exceptionally peaceful, with snow covering the ground. The sunsets were often stunning as the sun set behind the Blue Ridge Mountains. We also enjoyed hiking and exploring in Shenandoah National Park.

The Spirits in the Wind - Shenandoah National Park

On an early Saturday morning in mid-November 1995, I decided to go on an overnight hike. I planned to pack my gear into the backpack that Allison used on her European travels, but I soon realized it was too small for me. I needed a backpack to carry my few essential items: a tent, a camp stove, a pot, a flashlight, water bottles, an air mattress, food and an old sleeping bag.

I searched the Yellow Pages for a store that sold backpacks. The Appalachian Outfitter was located on Route 50, heading out of town. I arrived at the store around 10 a.m. I had no idea what size pack I needed, so I explained that I was heading to Shenandoah National Park. I bought a backpack and some dehydrated food, and I was on my way within an hour.

The entire event was poorly organized. While driving south on Skyline Drive in the park, I felt uncertain about where to start my journey. After traveling 25 miles south from the Front Royal entrance, I parked at a trailhead, still without a plan. Additionally, during hunting season, the park closed the entrance and exit gates at 5 p.m. Therefore, I needed to make sure I was back at the car by 4 p.m. on Sunday.

At approximately 2:00 p.m., I packed my gear into my backpack and began walking down the trail. My goal was to hike for several hours before finding a suitable place to set up my tent. Since Skyline Drive follows the park's ridgeline, all the trails descend from it. I hadn't encountered any other hikers on the path. As I continued, I realized no area was flat enough for my tent. My jeans and sweatshirt were drenched in sweat. Unlike today, I had no moisture-wicking clothing. I was pushing myself as dusk settled earlier in November. Finally, around six o'clock, I rounded a bend in the trail and found a flat spot to spend the night.

As the wind picked up and the temperature dropped, I quickly put on my jacket and set up the tent in the dark, relieved to have found a place to stay for the night. An hour later, while boiling water for dinner, I thought I heard voices coming down the trail, but no one appeared. As I ate, I kept listening to the sounds around me. I was surprised, having seen no one all afternoon. This time, it sounded like children laughing and playing as they passed by the trail. The noises were faint and blended with the wind, making me doubt their reality. I was sure no one was nearby; it was time to settle in for the night. The night sounds persisted: wind, rustling dry leaves, and the laughter and joy continued until late. Then, an eerie silence fell over the area.

My first camping trip in twenty years was cool and breezy, yet everything went smoothly. As I prepared breakfast in the early morning light, I noticed something unusual nearby—stones embedded in the ground. With a cup of coffee in hand, I investigated and found a small family plot with gravestones. The markers were weathered and lacked names or dates. I wondered who these individuals might have been and if I was hearing the spirits of children buried here long ago, before their families were relocated to form the national park. The emotions I felt were overwhelming, and I questioned what had happened the night before. Was it just the wind, or were those the voices of children resting in this peaceful place?

I walked around the area, wondering what life must have been like for families with so little flat ground. Families had lived in these hollows and steep drainages for generations until 1935, when the mountain residents were removed to create the national park. There was likely no electricity, running water, or access to education. It must have been challenging to make a living in such a remote and unforgiving place. As I explored, I found there might have been space for a small cabin, a garden, and a burial plot. I took photos of my tent, a deer that joined my camp, and some old family grave markers.

My task was to load my pack and return to the car before the gate closed. I will never forget the sounds I heard on that breezy November night in a hollow in the Blue Ridge Mountains.

Jackson Lake Lodge

On a calm, clear September morning at Jackson Lake Lodge during a meeting of the Western Governors Association in Jackson, Wyoming, I was admiring the view of the Grand Teton Range from the lodge patio. I had my camera with me, and Grand Teton Peak provided a stunning backdrop to Jackson Lake. In a few days, I would be climbing it. Having been at this very spot many times, I thought, "No, I don't need one more photo of the Grand Teton Peak." Then, Wyoming Governor Jim Geringer joined me at the great viewpoint. We had a brief exchange when he reached into his jacket pocket, pulled out a Kodak disposable camera, and started taking photos. My first thought was, "If the man who runs the state of Wyoming buys a disposable camera to capture this amazing view, then who am I to question it?" I reassessed my priorities and thought, of course, I could use one more photo of the Grand Teton Peak.

White House: Fourth of July and Christmas

In my first summer at NACo in 1986, we had a softball team that played in a league of Public Interest Groups (PIGs). This league included the US Conference of Mayors (USCM), the National League of Cities (NLC), the National Conference of State Legislatures (NCSL), the National Governors Association (NGA), and the National Association of Towns and Townships (NATaT). Our first game was held on the National Mall. I was playing third base, with the Washington Monument to my right, and as I looked toward home plate, the White House was just beyond Constitution Ave. That view was amazing to me, and a moment I will never forget. At that time, I was far from the softball game on the Rondout School diamond, surrounded by cornfields. Throughout the game, I was captivated by the sight of the Executive Mansion. I never imagined I would one day celebrate the nation's independence on the South Lawn of the White House.

On July 4, 1996, Trish was invited to spend the evening on the South Lawn, watching the National Mall fireworks with synchronized music. I was her plus one. We brought a blanket and sat on the lawn, enjoying food, drinks, music, people, and fireworks. An address from President Clinton capped the night. He had just returned from China and was joined on the balcony by Hillary, Al, and Tipper Gore. It was an unforgettable experience.

Because Trish was a Clinton appointee, we were always invited to tour the White House at Christmas. The White House holds a special place, but during the holiday season, its decorations, rich history, and architectural details become truly extraordinary. It is said that there are 165,000 holiday lights and 28,000 ornaments. Each year, we gave the White House Christmas Ornament as a gift. We appreciated it each time we visited. ¡Feliz Navidad!

Nelson Mandela and the Dalai Lama

After spending 27 years in prison, Nelson Mandela was released unconditionally in February 1990 and traveled to the United States. Trish and I were lucky enough to get tickets to witness this historic visit. Mandela's trip to Washington, DC, in June 1990 was an unforgettable moment for everyone present when he spoke.

The purpose was to thank the American people for their support during his years in prison. The delegation also aimed to impress upon the American people, the US President, and the US Congress the importance of opposing apartheid and maintaining sanctions against South Africa.

"Mandelamania" took America by storm in the summer of 1990. Tickets were in high demand. Velada Waller, who worked with Trish at the National Commission for Employment Policy, was then working for D.C. Mayor Marion Barry. That was the connection we needed to get tickets to witness that historic event. After meeting with President George H.W. Bush and addressing a joint session of Congress the following day, Mandela spoke to us at the packed Washington Convention Center.

Another memorable speaker was the Dalai Lama. Despite earlier speakers running over time, the Dalai Lama delivered an impressive and timely speech at the National Cathedral. With limited time, he skillfully adjusted his remarks, inspired us, and finished right on schedule.

Other memorable moments included seeing Mikhail Gorbachev at George Washington University, attending events with Presidents Ronald Reagan, Bill Clinton, and George H.W. Bush, nearly bumping into JF Kennedy Jr. at the White House Gatehouse, and meeting numerous senators, governors, and cabinet officials who shape the country.

The 100th Anniversary of Aaron Copland's Birth

The presidential election on November 7, 2000, signaled that Trish was nearing the end of her work with the Clinton administration. On November 14, we attended an evening event at the Kennedy Center to celebrate the 100th anniversary of Aaron Copland's birth. Recognized as the "Dean of American Composers" by peers and critics. We had excellent seats in President Clinton's box, although he was absent. Secretary Riley invited us to join. We've kept the M&Ms with the Presidential Seal for many years—maybe they are still in storage. The orchestra performed many of Copland's important works, with Speaker of the House Dennis Hastert narrating the event.

President's Council for Sustainable Development

In June 1993, President Clinton established the President's Council for Sustainable Development (PCSD) to advise his administration and to develop "bold, new approaches to achieve our economic, environmental, and equity goals."

I represented NACo on several work groups. The consensus was that local governments were perceived as the primary obstacle to sustainability. I never felt defensive because I knew many of the nation's 3,000 counties were doing exemplary work to protect the environment and encourage economic growth. Of course, it was not universal; however, that should be a goal of the PCSD. My recommendation to all was to involve local governments in the solution. At my suggestion, Randy Franke, the NACo president from Marion County, Oregon, was appointed to PCSD, while I took on the role of liaison. Vice President Al Gore served as the administration's primary point of contact, working closely with leaders of national environmental organizations, prominent business figures, various cabinet members, and local government officials.

NACo organized a coalition of local government organizations, including the National Association of Towns and Townships and the National League of Cities, to provide input to the PCSD. The testimony from elected officials of these groups to the PCSD was powerful. One memorable location for this exchange was during a meeting at the Presidio in San Francisco. We had six representatives testify: mayors, city council members, and county commissioners. One of our speakers was David Crockett, a Chattanooga city councilman. David's second great-granduncle was the frontiersman Davy Crockett. David and Randy Johnson, NACo President and Commissioner from Hennepin County, Minnesota, were among our top presenters. When we entered the room, the PCSD chair expressed concern about having too many speakers and reminded us that we only had 30 minutes.

We were ready for these guys. I told them it wouldn't be a problem. The goal was to have six elected officials speak, with a total time limit of 30 minutes. We prepared remarks for each speaker covering our main points. We did a run-through the night before the meeting when we arrived in San Francisco. The key was that no speaker could exceed four minutes.

Having assured the chair that we understood the time constraints, we promptly began and completed our testimony within 24 minutes. The committee was astonished and reminded us that we had more time.

We told them we were done. They assured us that the Council would carefully consider each point. They thanked us and said it would be wonderful if everyone were as organized as we were.

In 1994, the PCSD's first report recommended establishing a Joint Center for Sustainable Communities to create a partnership between NACo and the U.S. Conference of Mayors.

The Center was established and initially funded through grants from the Department of Housing and Urban Development and the Department of Energy. We identified examples of successful initiatives, hosted workshops, and published articles and case studies.

I was appointed as the administrator of the Joint Center. This collaboration led to the establishment of NACo's Smart Growth Initiative, which aimed to help county officials preserve the character and integrity of their communities and landscapes while ensuring local economic well-being. This initiative allowed NACo to identify best practices and disseminate them through workshops, conferences, and publications.

A Thank You from the Vice President

As I was wrapping up my work at NACo in 1999, I received a letter from Vice President Al Gore giving me a thumbs-up for my role in the PCSD. Part of the letter:

> *"Your vision, leadership, and commitment have been prominent since the President's Council on Sustainable Development (PCSD) was launched. You have worked tirelessly to make local government part of the solution and to bring the county perspective to the President's Council. Through your efforts, NACo's Sustainable Development Task Force presented critical viewpoints at key Council meetings. I especially appreciate your contributions to the development and recommendations of the PCSD's report, Sustainable America, which was given to the President in March 1996.*
>
> *Your reputation as a convener who works behind the scenes to make things happen and who can find common ground between diverse viewpoints and interests has served you and NACo well."*

Sincerely,
Al Gore
Vice President

Reading the vice president's letter brought to mind the traits my fifth-grade teacher, Virginia Matson, identified nearly 45 years previously.

June 30, 1984, Wedding Day

June 30, 1991, Marks our 27th anniversary.

1987, NACo

1992, Speaking at the Michigan Association of Counties

1990, With US Department of Labor Secretary Elizabeth Dole

1987, I was with US Department of Labor Secretary Bill Brock, Cliff Thomas, and Larry Jones.

1993, Making a point about the new legislation

THE COMMONWEALTH OF MASSACHUSETTS
EXECUTIVE DEPARTMENT
STATE HOUSE • BOSTON 02133

MICHAEL S. DUKAKIS
GOVERNOR

December 31, 1986

Jerald McNeil
Director of Employment and Training Programs
National Association of Counties
440 First Street, NW
Washington, DC 20001

Dear Jerry,

I wanted to thank you for the lead role you played in arranging my keynote address before the NACo Employment and Human Resources Conference in Fort Lauderdale, Florida.

It was a great pleasure and honor to speak to the group about Massachusetts' employment and training program for welfare recipients, ET Choices. As you may have been able to tell from my remarks, ET is a Massachusetts success story of which I am particularly proud and one which I hope will serve as a model as Congress considers ways to reform the present welfare system.

Moreover, I was grateful for the opportunity to meet with county officials in a more informal setting prior to my keynote address. The pre-luncheon meeting helped make for an enjoyable afternoon for Kitty and me.

Thanks again for all your hard work in putting together the conference. It was good talking with you.

Sincerely,

Michael S. Dukakis

1986, A Thank You from Massachusetts Governor Dukakis

1994, With Trish at the White House.

Nelson Mandela DC Welcoming Committee Presents

MANDELA

African National Congress Rally
Washington Convention Center
900 9th Street, NW, Washington, DC

June 26, 1990
Admission: $10.00

Doors open at 5:30 pm; Program begins at 7:00 pm
9TH STREET ENTRANCE ONLY
Seating Yellow Section Only

Chapter 13: Health Issues

Back Issues

The first part of my body to deteriorate was my back. I had been running on and off since I was fourteen. Then, in 1976, I started experiencing severe pain in my back and hips. After that, I could no longer run. In 1995, hiking and mountain climbing reignited my love for outdoor activities. However, at 53, I developed two herniated discs that caused permanent nerve damage in my lower left leg, leading to back surgeries in 1999 and 2002. With the support of an ankle brace, I was able to hike again, although nerve damage made it more difficult. Arthritis in my cervical vertebrae, along with a fall on the Nisqually Glacier on Mt. Rainier in 2003, resulted in periodic neck pain and headaches that lasted for seven years. I discuss this more in Chapter 18.

The construction work I undertook during my high school and college years may have contributed to some of my later physical ailments. The work was strenuous, and I lacked essential safety gear, including safety glasses and ear protection. Consequently, I have undergone three shoulder surgeries, two back operations, a hip replacement, two hip tendon reattachments, and hearing aids.

Nevertheless, I have climbed in the Rocky Mountains, the Cascade Mountains, Africa, South America, Mexico, Alaska, and Nepal. The imbalance between my left and right legs as a result of the nerve damage has caused numerous injuries and frustrations over the years. If I train too hard, I risk injury; if I don't train enough, I risk injury too.

In April 2024, I spent a week backpacking in the Grand Canyon with my longtime hiking buddy Doug Day. We hiked from the South Rim to the Colorado River, then up to the North Rim and back to the South Rim. This trip was the final challenge for my right hip. My left leg had been weak for 25 years, so my right leg had to compensate. After carrying that burden for so long, I needed a new hip. My right hip was replaced in December 2024.

Unfortunately, after eight months, my hip replacement surgery was not completely successful. After the operation and months of physical therapy, an MRI showed a full tear of the gluteus minimus tendon and a significant tear of the gluteus medius tendon, both needing surgery to repair. As I write this, my days of hiking and climbing might be over—I had surgery on September 5 to reattach these hip-stabilizing tendons. This will involve three to six months of rehab, but success isn't guaranteed. I hope to be walking without a cane again by 2026.

Depression

I've never written about my depression because it's a long story. Depression has been my biggest challenge. I've faced it at different times; it was a problem during my time at NIU, but it was especially intense in the 1980s and 90s. Luckily, Trish was incredibly understanding and supportive. In addition to the stress from my job in Washington, I dealt with episodes of depression and anxiety, as well as migraines. This struggle has had its ups and downs over time. As I mentioned earlier, the farm was a refuge for both of us while we navigated the weeks in DC. The holidays with kids from near and far were meaningful.

In the 1990s, I found success at NACo, but this increased my self-imposed stress and caused recurring episodes of depression. Over time, I struggled more with managing my accomplishments. Although I was performing well and received positive feedback from the Executive Director, I reached a breaking point in early 1999. My resignation caught many at NACo by surprise and disappointed others, including county officials and staff from federal departments.

In late 1998, Trish and I discussed finding a better place for myself and us. It wasn't Washington, D.C. Where else would I want to be? Colorado. We had visited Estes Park several times, but thought we needed to be closer to a big city, so we looked into Golden. It was near Denver, at the base of the Front Range. We weren't sure it was the right place, so we got creative and dreamed about living in a mountain town near a national park. We knew of a great spot—Estes Park. Maybe it was unrealistic, but we wanted to explore that option. In spring 1999, we found a wonderful place on the outskirts of town, just a short drive from the entrance to Rocky Mountain National Park (RMNP)—a three-bedroom house on 1.75 acres, surrounded by ponderosa pines, with large rocks and a meadow where elk often grazed.

Trish still had twenty-one months left as Assistant Secretary of Education in the Clinton Administration, so we decided I would stay in Colorado to recover. Meanwhile, Trish could continue her work in Washington.

Even though I was away from DC, I kept consulting for NACo on a project I started with the Sonoran Institute, the Western Community Stewardship Forum. I also had the chance to work at the Warming House, an outdoor outfitter, where I shared some of my knowledge of hiking and climbing.

Being alone in Colorado turned out to be a good thing for me. Although it was a difficult period, I realized I could experience depression without the weight of pretending to be happy. I often hiked in RMNP, which was nearly in my backyard. I frequently visited Alexandria, and Trish sometimes came to Estes Park. This arrangement lasted for almost two years. While I've moved past the worst, it hasn't completely gone away.

I visited many doctors and tried various medications for depression, but I seemed to be treatment-resistant. Spending time outdoors, like hiking and mountain climbing, has helped lift my mood. During this time, I was diagnosed with Attention-Deficit Hyperactivity Disorder, which might explain some of my academic struggles. I also take a mood-stabilizing medication. Even now, 25 years after leaving Washington, depression remains my constant companion.

Dealing with depression has been difficult and has affected my relationship with my children. Sometimes it's hard for me to reach out and communicate effectively. As I write and reflect on my life, I feel proud of what I have accomplished, but I also realize there is still much more I could accomplish. I try not to let those feelings discourage me.

Without a doubt, Trish supported me by offering the space I needed and by encouraging me. She continues to do so.

Chapter 14: Back to Colorado

New Home in Estes Park, Colorado

Because of my ongoing struggles with depression, I left my job at NACo. April 20, 1999, was a day I will never forget. After signing the paperwork for our new home in Estes Park, I was at the McDonald's Book Shop on Elkhorn Ave when the store radio broke the news of the Columbine Massacre in Littleton, Colorado. This event brought Sheriff John Stone of Jefferson County into the spotlight. I worked with John during his twelve years as a county commissioner in Jefferson County, where he served on several committees I staffed at NACo. Before becoming a county commissioner, he spent thirteen years as a police officer in Lakewood. He was elected sheriff in 1998 and served one term. Years later, he said, "This was my dream job, and it turned into a nightmare." I never knew the details of how he managed the massacre. I always saw John as someone who tried to do the right thing. But as he said, it was a nightmare. It remains one of the most infamous massacres in US history.

It took us about 21 months to settle into a new life together. We sold our property in the Shenandoah Mountains and moved our belongings to Estes Park. During this period, we kept an apartment in Alexandria, where Trish stayed for the rest of the Clinton administration, while I mainly lived in Estes Park.

As I was dealing with leaving my job, moving to Colorado, and selling the farm, I experienced severe pain in my back and left leg. After six months, it was determined that two herniated disks were causing the pain. In May, I had surgery in Fairfax, Virginia, and while lying in the hospital, I set a goal to reach the summit of Longs Peak by the end of the year. It's the highest point in RMNP at 14,259 feet and was clearly visible from the deck of our new home.

Climbing Longs Peak was a major challenge because I hadn't hiked or climbed for six months, and I had no idea what to expect. The good news was that I was walking again within weeks after surgery.

Unfortunately, the nerve damage in my left leg was permanent, and 25 years later, I am still experiencing the effects.

I started hiking with a friend, Jim Disney, a Larimer County commissioner in Colorado, where I lived. He introduced me to Howard Pomranka, a retired schoolteacher. Howard became a close friend and hiking partner. Both Jim and Howard grew up knowing each other in Loveland, also in Larimer County. Howard had summited all 54 of Colorado's 14,000-foot peaks. I relied on Howard's knowledge and experience. Howard wanted to help me reach my goal of climbing Longs Peak in 1999. We attempted it in late August, but high winds prevented us from reaching the summit. An early snowstorm in late September halted any attempt on the regular, relatively safe route. However, several weeks of warm weather followed, with no new snow. We thought there might still be a chance to reach the top. On November 16, we tried again. We hiked to the boulder field at 12,400 feet. As night fell, we spread out our bivy sacks and melted snow to fill our water bottles for the next day.

At six the next morning, I was getting ready to leave when Howard told me he wasn't feeling well and couldn't attempt the summit. Suddenly, I found myself on my own. Howard shared his knowledge with me, but he wouldn't be leading as planned. I was determined, so I grabbed some extra water and headed up to the Keyhole at 12,800 feet. Once through the Keyhole, there were supposed to be painted markers on the rocks along the ledges that led to the Trough, the Narrows, and then the Homestretch. Howard assured me I could find my way.

I found the route easily. However, my left ankle and foot had very little strength due to nerve damage, which caused a serious foot drop. The following year, I got an ankle brace, which made a significant difference. For now, I had to ensure that each step with my left foot landed on a flat rock or on one tilted inward. In November, with no other climbers around, I reached the top of the Trough at 13,900 feet. Then I saw someone starting up the Trough. I navigated the narrows alone—a 1,000-foot stretch with little elevation gain but a narrow spot about three feet wide and a 1,500-foot drop. I was nervous and tired, but I carefully made my way through the Narrows to the Homestretch. As I headed up the Homestretch, I saw the guy behind me catching up. He and I were the only people on the upper mountain, and my goal was to reach the top before him and start down quickly. If something were to happen to me, it would be good to have someone following. After a short stop at the top, I headed down and met the guy halfway down the Homestretch. We had a brief chat; he was a twenty-something from Boulder. I told him this was my first time, and I was alone, so I was glad to have someone trailing me on the way down.

I felt so relieved because he was very understanding. He said he would take his time at the summit and follow behind, but advised me not to rush. Five months after my back surgery, I managed to climb a 14,259-foot peak. I was exhausted, and the troublesome foot and ankle were a bother, but I still managed to get back to the Boulder Field to meet up with Howard. WOW! He was so happy to see I had made it, but even more relieved that I had come down safely. I climbed Longs Peak six more times. Many highs and lows have marked my climbing journey, the lows primarily due to age and injuries.

Road Trip to Colorado

On January 21, 2001, Trish finished her work in Washington, DC, after 37 years. We took a scenic route to Estes Park. Along the way, we visited Trish's Aunt Barbara Hinkson in Naples, Florida, and Aunt Connie Chase in Fort Myers. We also reached our fiftieth state: Arkansas for Trish and Alabama for me. Both of us have traveled extensively for work and have always enjoyed road trips and visits to national parks.

We loved Estes Park—it offered incredible hiking, snowshoeing, wildlife viewing, and breathtaking scenery (breathing already felt difficult at an elevation of 7,500 feet). We had a wonderful house with a view of Longs Peak, where elk and deer roamed freely in the yard. It was special when the children and grandchildren visited, and camping with the grandchildren was fantastic. We enjoyed some beautiful hikes with Trish's brother, Rocky, and his wife, Anja Chase—friends Jeff and Ann Wein from Denver, John Wallace and Ellen Rashbaum from San Francisco, and Chris Kulick from Maryland. Jeff was the CETA director for the City and County of Denver when I was the BOS/CETA director, and John worked with Trish at the National Commission for Employment Policy. Chris worked with both of us in Washington. We shared work histories in the fields of employment and training.

We were lucky to have neighbors who welcomed us, and we shared many meals. Our neighbor, Bill Pinkham, ran for Town Trustee, and Trish managed his campaign. He won and later served several terms as mayor.

Trish was consulting while we lived in Estes Park—this involved work trips across the country. I launched the Western Communities Stewardship Program before leaving Washington and continued working on the project remotely.

In 2003, we embarked on a significant renovation. Allison drew up plans for a new kitchen, dining room, flooring, and bookcases in the living room. We moved into the upstairs of Howard's house for six weeks. Allison ordered custom-built kitchen cabinets from Washington, and Richard and I rented a truck and drove them to Colorado. It was a big project, but the results were worth it.

Making a Movie

In 2001, the US National Park Service produced a film for the RMNP visitor center, intended as an introduction to the park. I was fortunate to have the chance to help and survive. The movie was called "Rocky Mountain National Park - Spirit of the Mountains." I assisted twice: once, we backpacked to Shelf Lake, which allowed the film crew to capture the sunset on Longs Peak in time-lapse; and on another day, I carried camera gear four miles to Timberline Falls. The setting was perfect, and the cameraman had plenty of great footage. However, Jason, the director, looked north and saw the dark, threatening clouds approaching Timberline Falls. He wanted to get some time-lapse footage of the storm approaching our location.

As it darkened and became more threatening, Jason knew time was running out. He wanted to stay as long as possible to capture the incredible footage, even if it meant risking all of us. Of course, we still had over four miles to return to the van. Jason asked me to hurry to the Bear Lake trailhead, retrieve the van, and drive down to the Glacier Gorge Trailhead to shorten the crew's trek. As I started my four-plus-mile dash, the hail began. I have never seen so much hail in my life. With the ominous sound of thunder and lightning flashing, I moved as quickly as I could.

There were five inches of hail and water underneath my feet, forming a small stream. The trail itself wasn't the problem; it was the lightning. Every year, several people die in RMNP from lightning strikes. As I traveled each mile, the frequency of lightning increased. I had to keep moving to reach the van and help the rest of the crew find safety. By the third mile, the hail had stopped; now it was just rain, thunder, and lightning. When I arrived at the Bear Lake Trailhead parking lot, the rain and threats persisted. I got in the van and headed to the Glacier Gorge Trailhead to rescue the rest of the film team. I arrived first and had to wait, hoping everyone was alright. As the minutes passed, my worry grew. Then, finally, they emerged from the trees and rushed to the van as quickly as they could. Everyone was safe.

As we headed toward the park headquarters, I sat next to Jason and asked if I would get any special recognition in the movie credits for saving everyone. He quickly replied, "No, only if you're struck by lightning." That got some laughs and eased the tense mood. I received a special thank-you in the film credits, along with others who volunteered. Be sure to watch to the very end (ha ha). You can now buy the movie on Amazon for $14.99.

Manila Clean Air Initiative

In June 2006, I traveled with a team from the United States to Manila, Philippines, to help implement the Clean Air Act. The Asian Development Bank (ADB) partnered with the US Environmental Protection Agency (EPA) to assist the Philippines in better managing this law. Two of the organizers were EPA staff members I had worked with previously at NACo. My primary role was to lead workgroups in developing strategies to involve the local community in addressing air quality issues.

My flight from New York to Tokyo passed over the Arctic Circle, where I witnessed an Arctic moonrise. It was a unique and unforgettable experience. I had seen the Northern Lights years ago; flying over the Arctic was just as memorable.

Manila's traffic was the scariest I've ever experienced. Drivers frequently use the wrong lanes and go against traffic to avoid congestion. The constant honking was overwhelming.

Our goal was to assist a nation and city in taking steps to cut pollution. Poverty levels are very high, and corruption is, admittedly, widespread. When we entered the ADB compound, security officers used mirrors on long poles to check the underside of our van because of a bombing at a rail station that had occurred the day before. Such civil unrest nearly led the ADB to cancel the workshop. Strict security measures enabled us to complete the three-day program safely. The Philippine participants found the information helpful; however, corruption remained the main obstacle to reducing pollution.

Some Great Memories

We have many wonderful memories from our time in Estes. Here are a few:

Sunday mornings featured blueberry pancakes at the Big Horn Cafe, followed by a scenic drive through RMNP, where we could sit and watch the elk graze. It was remarkably peaceful in winter when few people were around.

As we welcomed a new century, Trish had a brilliant idea: we should camp out in RMNP. That was different from what most people did. We cooked some stew we brought from home and settled into the tent. Knowing my dear partner is prone to getting cold, I had her slip into two sleeping bags. Trish was reading to me from *'Tuesdays with Morrie: An Old Man, A Young Man, and Life's Greatest Lesson,'* and I struggled to stay awake, nodding off several times. As midnight on December 31, 1999, approached, we left the tent and stood all alone on a nearby ridge to welcome the new century, just like we were in Times Square. We celebrated with a champagne toast, and as we did, a shooting star fell above Longs Peak. I will never forget where I was when we entered the 21st century. And it was a long way from the Dusty Road. By the way, the temperature dropped to fourteen degrees that night; however, we were prepared. Our first breakfast in the 21st century was cooked over a wood fire.

There was great excitement about the Leonid meteor shower in November 2001, one of the most notable meteor shower events of the early 2000s. We were prepared. We bundled up and waited on our deck. The shower finally began around midnight. When it started, meteors were falling in all directions. After half an hour, we grew cold and went inside. Even from inside, we could look out any window and still see the meteors. It was magical and something I will never forget. We were lucky to be in such a dark place, free from city lights, while the meteors rained down from the dark sky.

Together, we often hiked and snowshoed, climbing two 14,000-foot peaks: Mt. Elbert, Colorado's tallest mountain, and Longs Peak in RMNP. We also hiked twenty miles to Grand Lake along the Tonahutu Trail and stayed a couple of nights at the Rapids Lodge. Then we hiked eighteen miles along the North Inlet Trail, bringing our total to 38 miles. We did this twice.

An Elk at the Door

It was a gorgeous Sunday afternoon in early October, and the Broncos game at Mile High Stadium had just begun. Fall days in Estes Park can be breathtaking when the sky is a deep blue, and the aspen leaves are at their most vibrant. This was one of those perfect days. It was very quiet at 340 Meadow Circle. Trish was in Alexandria; I had gone on a great hike to Mills Lake that morning, and now John Elway and the Broncos were on TV – I felt like I was in my own special zone.

I was entirely focused on the game when I heard a faint knock at the front door. Before I could even get there, there was a series of quick knocks. So I thought, all right, all right, I'm on my way.

I opened the door and saw the decorative fall wreath that Trish had hung on the doorknocker. It had small cobs of Indian corn, but they were not on the door; instead, they were hanging from the mouth of a 600-pound elk. She was tall, over four feet at the shoulder. When she nipped at the wreath, the door knocker would bang.

I was stunned. Moments passed, and we both just stood there, our eyes locked, studying each other. It was incredible; I had never been that close to an elk. I spoke softly to her, and she listened while munching. Then I asked if she wanted to come inside. At that moment, she casually stepped back from the door, slowly turned around on the sidewalk, and calmly walked away, enjoying some corn on the cob.

My seven years in Estes Park were a transformative experience. Being surrounded by nature, free from pressure, and with lower expectations than at any other point in my life helped me significantly. This experience, combined with counseling and some mood-stabilizing medications, allowed me to emerge from a very dark period in my life.

Time to Say Goodbye to Estes Park

My struggles with depression changed while I was in Estes Park, but they were not over, and I felt Trish might be happier if she were in Seattle with Allison, Richard and their two children. We sold our wonderful house and left Estes Park in December 2006 to move to Seattle, Washington.

1999, Our Estes Park Home

2001, With Trish on the Summit of Longs Peak

The Crazy Horse Monument in 2003, 47 years after my first visit

2000, Elk in our yard

Chapter 15: On to the Pacific Northwest

Life in Seattle

Trish's daughter, Allison, and her husband, Richard Floisand, built a new house in Seattle in 2005. When it was finished, it included a separate basement apartment. Trish was working with an organization in Seattle and had to travel there occasionally. So, we rented the basement apartment in their new house to give her a convenient place to stay during her work trips. After moving from Colorado and downsizing from a three-bedroom house, we thought we would stay in the basement apartment, look at real estate, and recover from the move. The housing market was hot in 2007, and we couldn't find a property within our budget that didn't require a quarter of a million dollars in renovations before we could move in. So, we stayed in the apartment. It is now 2025, and we are still living there.

It allowed us to help Allison, Richard, Evan, and Anja over the years, giving us the freedom to travel. Shortly after moving, Trish enrolled in a postgraduate program in Education Policy and Leadership at the University of Washington. This was a heavy workload, and she earned her Master's Degree in 2015. Afterward, she mainly focused on genealogy and family history.

I joined the Mountaineers organization, where I met people I could go hiking and climbing with. I volunteered at the local food bank and resource center, and I also served on the board of directors. Hiking and climbing have been my passions for many years. They helped improve my outlook and keep my body active. Chapter 18 contains a lot of information about my outdoor adventures.

Before COVID, in our first years in Seattle, we were consistent about attending political debates and seeing prominent speakers, including Sandra Day O'Connor, Roger Mudd, Robert Reich, Isabel Wilkerson, Thomas Friedman, Daniel Schorr, and Mark Shields. We also attended history lectures at the University of Washington.

We weren't avid theatergoers, but we enjoyed good plays at the Seattle Rep, especially plays by August Wilson, who surprisingly spent his final decades in Seattle. We also enjoyed trips to Semiahmoo Lodge, the San Juan Islands, Seabrook Beach, Quinault Lodge, and Kalaloch Lodge in Olympic National Park. We visited Cannon Beach in Oregon and attended the Shakespeare Festival in Ashland, Oregon, twice.

During the COVID-19 pandemic, we kept in touch with friends across the country through Zoom. Unfortunately, we've fallen out of the habit.

Planes, trains, and automobiles

I have really enjoyed reconnecting with my LHS friends over the past ten years. Since our fiftieth reunion in 2014, we have had three more gatherings at the homes of my close friends Bill Huxhold and Susan Fisher, a couple who own two neighboring houses on a lake in Elkhorn, Wisconsin. For us, the 2014 reunion started with a 44-hour Amtrak train trip to Chicago. The 50th LHS reunion was so enjoyable that we celebrated our 70th birthdays with a reunion in 2016, an impromptu gathering in 2022, and another for our 60th LHS reunion in 2024. All of the classmates who attend feel lucky to have grown up in Libertyville when we did. Bill and Susan hosted the very best reunions, it’s true.

Along with our travels in the US, Trish and I have enjoyed many trips to Europe, including sailing from Paris to the beaches of Normandy, exploring Greece and the Aegean Islands, sailing around the British Isles, and visiting England, Scotland, Wales, Ireland, France, Germany, Italy, Austria, Turkey, Mexico, and Australia.

Two of my favorite trips include cruising down the Seine River from Paris to Normandy and exploring the British Isles by ship. The first trip started in Paris and included many villages and historic sites, such as a visit to Giverny, Claude Monet's home and gardens; Conflans, where Van Gogh spent his final months painting; a hike uphill to Château Gaillard in Les Andelys; and Rouen, home to the Joan of Arc Museum. Visiting Normandy’s beaches and cemeteries was like stepping back in time, but it was still hard to fully grasp the destruction and sacrifice of that era.

Our trip to the British Isles was highlighted by the presence of Trish's brother, Rocky Chase, and his wife, Anja. Oh, another highlight besides Rocky, we saw Queen Elizabeth II reviewing her honor guard at Holyrood Palace. We started in Edinburgh, Scotland, then traveled north to the Orkney Islands, Belfast in Northern Ireland, and Dublin in Ireland. We also spent a day on Barra, the southernmost island of Scotland's Outer Hebrides, known for Kisimul Castle, the ancestral home of the Clan MacNeil. This 15th-century castle is the only major medieval castle still standing in the Outer Hebrides. Additionally, we explored the mountains and castles of Wales. It was twelve incredible days, each filled with new adventures.

These travels, along with my climbing trips to Argentina, Ecuador, Mexico, Alaska, Nepal, and Tanzania, and a business trip to Manila, have allowed me to wander as my grandfather did.

We also enjoy watching baseball, football, film noir, and British mysteries, as well as working on our genealogy.

Selfie Instruction from Bill Clinton

I've never been good at taking selfies. This became clear to Bill Clinton, who offered some advice. In August 2018, Trish and I attended a fantastic event celebrating the installation of Governor Richard Riley's collection in the South Carolina Political Collections at the University of South Carolina Libraries. President Bill Clinton was the main speaker. After the formal program, a private reception was held for former US Department of Education staff who worked with Dick Riley during his eight years as Secretary. We had hoped President Clinton would stop by the reception. Just when we thought he wouldn't come, he showed up. Everyone was trying to get a photo of him or with him, thinking he might leave suddenly.

The excitement for taking photos faded, and then Clinton mingled with people, even going behind the bar to have his picture taken with the bartenders. By this time, everything was very relaxed. I was talking to the President and asked if I could take a selfie with him. He was happy to, but I was fumbling, so he kindly took my phone and showed me how to extend my arm and hold the phone at the right height. This was a man who had been in thousands of selfies and knew what he was doing. I listened and watched as he demonstrated. Looking at the photos now, it doesn't look like I was an outstanding student. He looks great, but I look like I'm straining to get a good selfie. I understood the part about holding the phone, but not the part about smiling. He made it look so easy.

A Sigma Alpha Epsilon Brother

One Saturday morning at the Rugged Acres, I was leafing through the Sigma Alpha Epsilon (SAE) fraternity magazine "The Record" when I suddenly came across a picture of Trish's boss, Dick Riley. Many prominent SAE brothers exist, but I have never personally met any of them. Brother Riley was a two-time governor of South Carolina and served two terms as Secretary of Education in the Clinton Administration. In the days that followed, Trish told the Secretary about our shared fraternity connection. After that, whenever we met, it was always the fraternity grip and greeting, "Phi Alpha." At his 90th birthday celebration, I was honored to present him with an extraordinary citation from the SAE Supreme Council, recognizing and congratulating Dick on his lifetime of service and for being a True Gentleman. In SAE, *the True Gentleman is the man whose conduct proceeds from goodwill... whose deeds follow his words... who considers the rights and feelings of others... a man for whom honor is sacred and virtue is kept safe.*

"Phi Alpha" Brother Riley

Floisand Studio Architects (FSA)

In April 2007, Allison and her husband Richard asked me to join their architectural firm, Floisand Studio, as the office manager. I worked in the office for several years, but eventually I preferred working remotely. Richard would bring home the bills and customers' payments, and I would process the checks and make deposits. I used QuickBooks for bookkeeping and assisted in drafting bylaws and corporate policies.

My responsibilities included processing payroll, filing all related federal and state quarterly and annual employee tax reports, preparing customer invoices, making deposits, and submitting incorporation documents to the Secretary of State. I also prepared and filed annual reports, ensuring that state and city licenses remained current. During the COVID-19 pandemic, I assisted Allison in securing support for small businesses through the Small Business Administration.

Making payroll on the 25th of each month was sometimes challenging in places like Santa Margarita, Italy, and Manchester, United Kingdom, as well as many other cities across the country. The time difference and technology often led to frustrating experiences.

I served for sixteen years and eight months until January 2024, when I handed over my responsibilities to Allison. She hired someone to handle specific tasks, while she and Richard took on additional duties. Now, I'm retired.

2009, John Wallace, Ellen Rashbaum, and Trish at San Francisco Bay.

2013, With Trish on the Acropolis in Athens.

2015, With Trish in Paris,

2017, Standing next to the John Lennon statue outside the Cavern Club in Liverpool, UK,

2017, With Trish visiting the ancestral home of the MacNeill clan in Castle Bay, Barra, Scotland.

2017, With Rocky & Anja Chase, and Trish in London

2018, With Trish

2023, At the statue of Sigma Alpha Epsilon brother Dick Riley in Greenville, South Carolina

2024, At St. Maximin Church in Koblenz, Germany, where my great-grandfather, Anton Seyl, was baptized.

2023, Sigma Alpha Epsilon brother, former South Carolina Governor Dick Riley's 90th birthday, Greenville, South Carolina

2024, Celebrating 40 years of marriage in Bamberg, Germany

Chapter 16: Odds and Ends

Failure to Communicate

Alamosa is situated in the San Luis Valley of southern Colorado. The high mountain valley is at an elevation of 7,500 feet and extends roughly 74 miles in both length and width. For many years, the Alamosa JCs distributed free coffee and donuts at the top of the pass on Memorial Day, the Fourth of July, and Labor Day. We did this to promote safety, making it a considerate gesture for travelers visiting the valley. As External Vice President, coordinating this project was among my duties.

Memorial Day had perfect weather, and our goal was to have everything ready at the top of the pass by 9:00 a.m. We had to stay organized because the rest stop was 67 miles from Alamosa. Everyone had their assignments: coffee urns, sugar, creamers, cups, napkins, tables, chairs, signs, and the donuts. The donuts were Sudnuts. Somehow, potatoes were included in the mixture. The San Luis Valley was a major producer of potatoes. Everyone knew their roles and was expected to arrive by 8:30 a.m. to set up and be ready by 9:00 a.m.

We were all there by 8:30, except for the donuts. Where was Bill? At nine o'clock, we started serving coffee and apologized for the lack of donuts, even though the sign indicated they were available. Of course, there were no cell phones in 1972, and we hoped Bill would arrive soon and be okay. Ten o'clock passed, and he still hadn't shown up. Finally, at noon, Bill came, dragging himself into the rest area. He was apologetic and a bit exhausted.

Hooray, the Sudnuts arrived, and we had happy travelers. Some of our team members were a little upset by Bill's late arrival. Not wanting to sound too accusatory, I politely asked, "Bill, what happened that you didn't make the 9 a.m. start time?"

Timidly, Bill explained, "I arrived on time, reaching the top of the pass at 8:30 as instructed, but no one was there. I waited, expecting everyone to arrive by nine. When it was 9:30 and still no one was in sight, I began to worry. The traffic on La Veta Pass was picking up, and I was alone. Then I realized I might be on the wrong pass and hurried here to Wolf Creek Pass; it was over a hundred miles from La Veta Pass. I drove as fast as I could to get here."

From then on, it was no longer just "Top of the Pass," but specifically "Top of Wolf Creek Pass."

Working with Governor Lamm

My first visit to the governor's office was an exciting experience. I had previously visited the Colorado Capitol in 1956 when I was just a ten-year-old tourist. Later, in 1971, as a state employee, I often walked to the Capitol during my lunch break to admire the beautiful murals, marble, and stained glass, and I was amazed by the door marked "Governor." I never thought I would get the chance to step inside that office, let alone meet the governor there.

The passive solar training and installation project I mentioned earlier resulted in a 30-minute training video. This was a significant effort, and we wanted Gov. Lamm to narrate it. His office approved. We worked on the script and prepared to schedule a filming date and location with the governor. Our first choice was the cliff dwellings at Mesa Verde National Park, where we hoped to show that the Anasazi had used passive solar design for centuries. Unfortunately, that plan was not feasible because the governor didn't have time to travel to southwestern Colorado. Our second option was to film at Red Rocks Park and Amphitheater, located in the foothills west of Denver, but that proved too time-consuming as well. Our third choice was the camel enclosure at the Denver Zoo. This worked out, but the truck noise from nearby Colorado Blvd caused many retakes. This is Part One of the story.

Part Two: Governor Lamm served from 1974 to 1986 and was known for being prickly. People were cautious around him. After the movie was finished, we wanted to show it to the Governor before anyone else had a chance to see it. The screening would take place in his office when he returned from an event, giving us time to set up the projector and test the equipment. My boss, Bob Ore, a member of the Governor's cabinet, was with me. We had everything ready when the projector bulb burned out. We didn't have a spare.

I asked the Governor's secretary if I could use the Governor's phone to contact my office, and she agreed. I called, but unfortunately, no projector bulb was available. We felt a bit anxious because the Governor was on a tight schedule and would soon return, expecting to watch the movie. Bob, a former state legislator, went to the Legislative Affairs office in the Capitol basement to search for a bulb. While I was making another call on the Governor's phone behind his desk, he walked in through a side door with his state patrol security officer. It was pretty uncomfortable being behind his desk, on his phone! He gave me a disapproving look. Fortunately, Bob returned with the bulb we needed just in time. We explained the situation to the Governor and reassured him that we'd be ready shortly. The Governor stepped out to speak with his secretary while we finished our preparations. Eventually, we started the movie without popcorn or jokes. He seemed to be in a bad mood, and I was worried he might find the film disappointing. However, he looked great in his plaid flannel shirt. He thought it was fantastic and appreciated the chance to support our passive solar initiative. I often joked that I avoided wearing my gray three-piece, pin-striped suit around the Governor because it might remind him of that guy standing behind his desk using his phone.

Uncovering Fraud

In late summer 1983, at 10:00 a.m., two members of my Internal Monitoring Unit arrived with alarming news. They had just returned from the State Treasurer's Office, where they uncovered a serious issue. During their review of State Warrants (similar to checks) charged to our accounts, they found discrepancies: our fiscal officer had forged the signatures of my boss and me on warrants for himself, his family, and fictitious individuals. The evidence was irrefutable.

Since I had never encountered fraud at work, this was new territory for me. I quickly took steps to address the situation.

Step one: I called Jim, our fiscal officer, into my office, showed him the evidence, and he admitted to the fraud. I then placed him on administrative leave while further investigations were carried out. Step two: I drove to South Denver to inform my boss, Ruben Valdez, the Executive Director of the Department of Labor and Employment, who was attending a business meeting there, about the situation. He agreed with my decision. Step three: I went to the Denver District Attorney's Office to file a report. Step four: After returning to my office, I contacted the US Department of Labor's Office of the Inspector General in Dallas to report the issue.

By 4 p.m., I was feeling like I had just survived a tornado. On a positive note, I received recognition for uncovering the embezzlement, which I credited to the Internal Monitoring Unit's staff. As it turned out, Jim was terminated and prosecuted. He had been doing a good job, but his problem was gambling debts.

Meeting Darth Vader

On a Saturday morning in 1983, I heard Darth Vader's voice while waiting in the checkout line at King Soopers grocery store in Denver. I wasn't paying attention to the people around me, but James Earl Jones was speaking right in front of me, chatting with the cashier. What an incredible voice! He had been in town to see his sister perform in a theater production the night before. What a way to start the day! Not being a Star Wars fan, I mistakenly said, "May the force be with you." I didn't realize that Darth Vader didn't say that. His response was, "Don't underestimate the power of the force."

I wish I had remembered to mention his lines as Terrance Mann in Field of Dreams: "The one constant through all the years, Ray, has been baseball. America has rolled by like an army of steamrollers. It's been erased like a blackboard, rebuilt, and erased again. But baseball has marked the time."

But instead, I just said, "Have a nice day."

Chapter 17: Baseball Stories

First Trip to Wrigley Field

It was a Saturday in mid-May, sunny and warm, spring in Illinois. Those were beautiful days, with the grass a vibrant green and the spring flowers in full bloom. (Though I wasn't fond of flowers then, I loved baseball!) The Braves had left Boston in 1953 and played in Milwaukee to the north, while the Cubs and Sox were to the south. My only experience with baseball was at Bradley Road Stadium, which had a gravel driveway, telephone lines, electrical wires, and an old-fashioned garage door—conditions that meant the tennis ball could fly chaotically in any direction. To me, this was my Yankee Stadium. I spent hours there with my tennis ball. Since I was in the country, there weren't many worthy opponents nearby—none within a mile—so I was the star of my own ballpark.

But that Saturday in 1955 was about to change everything forever, and it is a day I can never forget. I was outside in the driveway with my tennis ball when Hugh McKay from down the road drove into our gravel driveway in his new 1955 Chevy Bel Air. It was green and white, but lacked the classic lines introduced in 1957. Mr. McKay had stopped to talk with my father about something. He got out of the car and stood by our back door, talking to Dad. Then it happened! Almost as an afterthought, he said, "I am taking Jimmy and Steve Hieser down to Wrigley Field to see the Cubs play the Giants. Do you think Jerry would like to come along?" I froze. I did not want to disturb my father's ability to think clearly. I had never been to a big-league ballpark before. I had only been to Chicago once, and that was at Christmas to look at the windows on State Street and see Santa at Marshall Fields—but now Wrigley Field! I wanted to shout for joy. I strained to hear the answer to the most important question of my whole life. Then I listened to the "yes" and threw my tennis ball high in celebration!

My dad pulled out his wallet, which was resting deep in the pocket of his khaki pants. He handed Mr. McKay a dollar to cover my expenses for the day and told me, "Have a good time, do what Mr. McKay tells you, and be careful." Just like that, we headed down the dusty gravel road to a big-league baseball game. Hugh McKay was a plumber who always looked like he'd just stepped out of the shower and put on a fresh set of clothes, kind of like Ozzie Nelson. He always appeared neat and loved baseball, having volunteered as a coach for years. He knew his baseball, while I didn't know much. TV was still pretty new, and our only radio was tuned to news and talk on WKRS from Waukegan.

My baseball knowledge was limited to recognizing that a home run occurred when I threw a tennis ball that hit the garage door handle and flew over the high telephone wire. I was sure Wrigley Field had neither garage doors nor telephone wires, so I had a lot to learn. Jimmy and Steve, two years older than I, seemed to know everything about baseball. They talked about things I didn't understand, like "Hank Sauer will powder one today. I hope Banks hits a grand slam. Bob Rush will fool them with his change of pace." What were they talking about?

I listened intently to every word, as if I had been deprived of this crucial information for far too long. They mainly discussed Hank Sauer and dreamed of catching a foul ball hit by his bat. I had never heard of Hank Sauer, despite his hitting 44 homers in '54. However, I was familiar with the shortstop Ernie Banks, who was in his second season with the Cubs. I hoped to learn more. Who were these New York Giants, anyway? They're World Champs, don't you know? They swept Cleveland last year. Don't you remember that amazing catch by Willie Mays? Well, maybe I did remember it. I was feeling a bit foolish and decided not to ask any more questions.

Before long, we drove down Waveland Avenue toward Sheffield Avenue, and my first view of Wrigley Field was the back of the scoreboard. I wasn't impressed. The guys were confident that Hank would hit one over the right-field wall, but I said nothing.

As we entered the ballpark, each of us received a scorecard. It cost only ten cents and was just a simple card with the team rosters on one side and the scorecard on the other. As we walked up the ramp to our seats, I finally saw the field. Wow! The grass was the greenest green I had ever seen. Things were getting exciting—going from the Bradley Road ballpark in the morning to Wrigley Field in the afternoon. I had never imagined experiencing something like this. I sat there watching players warm up, take batting practice, catch fly balls, run, and play catch. I watched until I couldn't wait any longer, then asked, "How can you tell which team is which?" Boy, what a silly question. Of course, everyone knows the Cubs are the home team and wear white, while the

Giants are visitors in gray. It all made sense. Still, it was strange to see grown-ups in baseball uniforms. I had thought baseball players were just big kids, but it was obvious these men weren't.

Before I knew it, the game was underway—Sal "the Barber" Maglie pitched for the Giants, and Bob Rush for the Cubs. It felt like a blur. This game was different from the ones I was used to. Who was Lippy Leo, anyway? Could he catch a fly off the high telephone wire? That's a tough catch. I didn't understand what was happening, but I knew this was more significant than Marshall Field's at Christmas. This was the big time. It was my first Saturday at the ballpark—the ivy walls, Ernie Banks, Willie Mays, Mr. Durocher, Gene Baker, Alvin Dark, Hoyt Wilhelm, and Ransom Jackson. At nine years old, I suddenly fell in love with baseball.

It ended too quickly. The game was over—the Cubs won eight to nothing—with no foul ball for Jimmy or Steve. I found out that Lippy Leo didn't catch fly balls off telephone wires (I met Leo Durocher and Willie Mays thirty years later). He was the guy from New York who argued with everyone. Before I knew it, we were heading back home to the Dusty Road, which was my world and would never be the same after that day in May.

White Sox in the Playoffs

The Chicago White Sox were my favorite baseball team when I was a kid. The White Sox lost the infamous 1919 World Series to the Cincinnati Reds. Afterward, a few players from the White Sox were accused of throwing the series. The team suddenly became known as the Black Sox. The players were cleared in court, but nine of them were permanently banned from baseball by the Commissioner, Judge Kenesaw Mountain Landis.

The White Sox endured a 40-year wait before they reached the World Series in 1959, only to lose to the LA Dodgers four games to two. I was crushed. Twenty-four years later, they reached the American League playoffs with a shot at the World Series. On October 5, 1983, they played against the Baltimore Orioles. Trish and I tried to get tickets for the game, but we were unsuccessful. Luckily, a friend helped us. Her ex-husband, who worked for NBC Sports, managed to get us three tickets. These tickets, however, were unusual because they included letters and numbers for sections that didn't match any regular seats at Memorial Stadium in Baltimore. We had no idea where we would be sitting and wondered whether it would be in the bleachers or on a special bench.

Beth Buehlmann joined us, and we had a late start, leaving D.C. When we reached the stadium and entered through the main gate, we were directed to the third-base side and then guided toward the field. An expanded section made of plywood held three rows of folding chairs along the third-base side, between the on-deck circle and the Orioles' dugout. This was unbelievable; not only were we in that section, but we also had seats in the first row. We were in shock.

As we sat there, we had to stand up to let Lee MacPhail, president of the American League, and Missouri Senator Tom Eagleton pass by. He was the Vice Presidential nominee chosen to run with George McGovern in 1972, until he withdrew. Wow! This was incredible. Before the game started, I asked Lee MacPhail to sign a baseball I had brought. He graciously signed it after we had a quick chat.

This was fantastic; now let's watch a baseball game. Since the on-deck circle was directly in front of us, we took great photos of Eddie Murray, Al Bumbry, Rick Dempsey, and a rookie named Cal Ripken, Jr. What could make this day even more memorable? A White Sox win and catching a foul ball.

The White Sox won 2-1, and Tippy Martinez pitched two innings for the Orioles. Tippy had been part of the CETA Summer Youth program when I was heading it in Pueblo, Colorado. Tippy was from La Junta and returned many times over the years to speak to the program participants.

In the fifth inning, Tom Paciorek, the White Sox first baseman, hit a dribbling foul ball toward our section. As it got closer, I thought I had a chance to reach it. I missed, and it hit the plywood wall, then bounced back toward the field. I leaned a little further over the wall to try to grab it as it bounced away. I think Beth and Trish grabbed my feet so I wouldn't land on the field. Success. The ball was now mine.

That was a great day. But the White Sox lost the next three games, and the season ended. A small comfort was that Tippy Martinez, the kid from the CETA Youth program, was the winning pitcher in the final game.

Headline news: Chicago's Tom Paciorek (#44) had two hits, an RBI, a walk, and a dribbler to Jerry McNeil.

Baseball's Immortals

Charles M. Conlon was one of the most renowned photographers of baseball's golden era. He captured thousands of images of baseball greats, including Ty Cobb, Babe Ruth, Joe DiMaggio, Ted Williams, and Lefty Gomez, among many others. Throughout his career, Conlon created at least 30,000 images from 1904 to 1941. In October 1984, the Smithsonian National Portrait Gallery hosted an exhibition of his work. Naturally, invitations were sent to many of the players he had photographed. However, forty years after his retirement, many players were deceased, ill, or otherwise occupied. Fortunately, three Hall of Famers attended the opening: Leo "the Lip" Durocher, Bill Terry (the last man to hit .400 in the National League in 1930), and Lefty Gomez (the starting pitcher for the American League in the first three All-Star games).

I was working on *"Baseball In the News, Classic Movie Theater Newsreels."* Baseball history fascinated me, and I was especially interested in seeing the most famous photographs from that history. So, Trish and I headed to the National Portrait Gallery. Little did I know that I would meet a baseball legend with whom I would eventually spend many captivating hours.

As we made our way up a flight of marble stairs, enormous blowups of baseball legends came into view. One featured a massive poster of Babe Ruth swinging at a ball and watching it soar through the air. Inside, the images were displayed on the walls, from the ceiling, and on easels.

We immersed ourselves in images of baseball's immortals. Conlon's most enduring photograph from 1910 features Ty Cobb sliding into third base with dirt flying. It is regarded as one of the earliest action photographs ever taken.

After half an hour of studying legendary baseball players from before my time, the program began. A good-sized crowd had gathered, but it wasn't too crowded. Paul McFarlane, the historian for *The Sporting News*, served as the master of ceremonies and delivered the opening remarks, introducing the exhibit "Charles M. Conlon, the man and his life's work". After the presentations, it was time to welcome the special guests. Each Hall of Fame member was introduced and seated at a table to sign autographs. The Smithsonian cleverly produced a collection of one hundred oversized baseball cards featuring Conlon's images. Trish and I bought a card for each player present. Then, armed with two baseballs, we joined the lines to meet three "baseball immortals." Not knowing how long they would be available, we split up to quickly say hello and get signatures. The lines were short, but I felt like a ten-year-old eager to make sure all of my items were signed.

Before long, we moved from one line to the next. With two people, three lines, and a man acting like a ten-year-old, I accidentally gave Trish the wrong ball when she approached Leo Durocher for an autograph. Leo looked for a spot to sign and said, "I've already signed this, sweetheart." Trish remains eternally embarrassed. Perhaps his tone could have been more forgiving. Yet, it is a moment that we still laugh about many decades later.

I didn't have to worry about getting all the signatures. The crowd was manageable, and the men enjoyed the spotlight once again. After the signing concluded, they wanted to experience the exhibition themselves.

This event turned out to be a fantastic opportunity. As the dignitaries explored the exhibition, I had the chance to speak with them. Consequently, I established two important contacts: Paul McFarlane, whom I would later visit at his office at *The Sporting News* in St. Louis, and Hall of Famer Lefty Gomez, with whom I would share a beer and breakfast (not beer at breakfast) two months later.

I spent most of my time with Lefty Gomez; we discussed the photographs, especially a famous Babe Ruth portrait where he had just taken a big swing and the ball was on its way out of the park. Babe is looking up into the sky, following the ball. It has always looked like a home run to me. But Lefty says, "If you look at that, Babe is looking almost straight up, you know that's just a pop-up. It won't get out of the infield." Doggone it! He was right, and I'll never see that picture the same way again.

Winter Baseball Meetings

In December 1984, I attended the Major League Baseball winter meetings at the Hyatt Regency Hotel in Houston, Texas. I assisted with the Denver Baseball Commission's booth in the exhibit hall. The commission was promoting Denver as a potential expansion city for Major League Baseball. Steve Katish, the commission's executive director and someone I knew from Denver, invited me to showcase *"Baseball in the News"* at the booth. This was Volume I of the video series of movie theater newsreels produced by my company, Great American Pastimes. This was the first opportunity to share it with the public.

The Denver Baseball Commission booth was busy most of the time. Many retired ballplayers were captivated by the newsreels. Denver had to wait another nine years before the Colorado Rockies played their first game at Mile High Stadium in 1993. In the club's first season, attendance reached 4,483,350 over 79 home dates (81 games – two doubleheaders), averaging 56,751 attendees per game—a Major League single-season attendance record.

During meetings, I carried a letter of introduction from Chuck Stevens, Secretary of the Professional Baseball Players Association of America (PBPA). He kindly wrote this letter in early 1984 when I visited him in Garden Grove, California. It enabled me to mention his name to gain endorsements from some Hall of Fame baseball players. More about Chuck appears in the *Baseball in the News* section of Chapter 12.

The first time I used that letter was at the winter baseball meetings for team owners and executives. The Detroit Tigers had just won the World Series, and Sparky Anderson, the Tigers' manager, was on his way to a live TV interview. Before he started the interview, I told him about Chuck's support and asked him to endorse *Baseball in the News.* He said, "Absolutely, I want you to write something up while I'm doing the interview, OK?" While he was on live TV, I stood behind the camera, creating a quote for him. When Sparky finished the interview, he quickly left the area. He forgot to review the quotation and sign the release. When I caught up to him, he was apologetic, took the time to review what I had written, and signed the release form. Sparky Anderson was my first endorsement.

On the second evening of the meetings, a special dinner was held on the floor of the Houston Astrodome. The Astrodome was the first indoor baseball stadium. Its doors opened in 1964. Buses picked us up from the hotel. A remarkable array of well-known ballplayers attended. Tommy Lasorda was bustling around the lobby, greeting various guests. Pete Rose wore a blue warm-up suit, exuding his typical air of superiority.

Meanwhile, Gene Autry, owner of the California Angels, patiently stood by the door, waiting. I stood next to him, also waiting. What do you say to someone who was a childhood idol? How have you been? How are the meetings going? *Frosty the Snowman* was one of my favorites. Would you sing a verse or two? I was so starstruck that all I managed to say was, "Hello, good to see you."

When we were at the Astrodome, my table was located near where third base would usually be. The whole floor was covered with Astroturf to accommodate other events. I don't remember anything particularly remarkable. It was nice to admire the structure and observe the attendees. I had chicken in the Houston Astrodome—such a long way from my days at the Libertyville Little League banquet.

The Topps Beer Garden

Hall of Fame pitcher Bob Lemon stopped by the booth, and we had a great conversation. Later, I headed over to the Topps Baseball Card beer garden. Bob noticed me and invited me to join him and several Major League scouts at his table. Bob Lemon was a Hall of Fame pitcher for the Cleveland Indians in the 1940s and '50s. He later managed the Chicago White Sox and led the New York Yankees to a World Series victory in 1978. He was named American League Manager of the Year twice. Just sitting there and listening was a fantastic opportunity.

He discussed starting his career at third base with the Cleveland Indians in 1941. During World War II, he served in the Navy and played baseball. He mainly played third base but also practiced pitching. The U.S. Military played baseball during World War II primarily to boost morale for troops and civilians and to support the war effort. Baseball also supported the war effort through activities such as selling war bonds and fundraising. In 1946, the Indians already had a third baseman, so the manager moved Bob to center field because of his strong throwing arm. Unfortunately, Bob struggled to hit the change-up and lost his spot in center field. However, Indians manager Lou Boudreau remembered Bob's Navy pitching experience and let him pitch. By mid-1947, he had become one of Cleveland's best pitchers. He said his time in the Navy was a stepping stone to a successful baseball career.

Bob told me that his best job was teaching Ronald Reagan to pitch for the 1952 film *"The Winning Team."* The film starred Reagan as Hall of Fame pitcher Grover Cleveland Alexander, while Lemon portrayed the future Hall of Fame pitcher Jesse “Pop” Haines.

He would head to the Warner Bros. lot each morning, where he and Ronald Reagan would spend half an hour throwing a baseball. Lemon was primarily focused on helping Reagan achieve a smooth windup and a natural follow-through. He said that teaching someone to look like a veteran pitcher was quite challenging. Reagan practiced diligently, but being a busy actor, there wasn’t enough time to truly resemble the seasoned pro Alexander.

Lemon noted that it was pretty cold in the early winter mornings, even in Southern California. However, by 9:00 a.m., he had completed his pitching instruction and left the studio lot to play golf across the street. He thought that was easy money.

He discussed traveling by train as a valuable experience during the 1940s and 1950s. “Reflecting on the games we had just played provided a great learning opportunity.” These conversations often occurred among players. Critiquing a teammate was challenging, and receiving criticism was even more so. However, the long train rides allowed time to transition into these discussions after the heat of the moment had passed.

The give-and-take enhanced camaraderie among team members. However, the longer trips required spending up to twenty hours on the train, in cramped spaces, and with the train needing to switch tracks through the night.

He compared his experience to the 1980s, when most games were played at night; after each series, it was off to the airport to catch a flight and arrive in the next city at 3:00 a.m. The fatigue and time pressure were such that players did not have the chance to replay game situations. He also believed that players in the 1980s faced more pressure than those in the 1940s and '50s.

He mentioned that the heat and humidity were nearly unbearable when traveling to the Midwest in July and August. The lack of air conditioning on trains and in hotels contributed to a long, sweltering summer. Moreover, St. Louis was one of the most challenging cities to play in. The Browns and Cardinals shared Sportsman's Park, which was in poor condition by August. The grass in the outfield was patchy and in the worst shape of any field in the major leagues. Life became more manageable in the 1950s when Chase Park Plaza in St. Louis finally added air conditioning.

In 1954, the St. Louis Browns relocated to Baltimore, leaving Chicago as the westernmost American League city. As a result, there were no more American League games in St. Louis, but the National League's Cardinals had the field to themselves.

Bob shared wisdom as we parted: "Two important things in life are good friends and a great bullpen."

Having a drink with Hank Aaron

One evening, the Washington D.C. Baseball Commission hosted a reception in one of the hotel ballrooms. Major league players, managers, team staff, and folks like me filled the room. Several rolling bars were set up, and I made my way to the nearest one. As I approached, I noticed Hank Aaron, baseball's home run king, standing there trying to get a drink. The young bartender struggled to serve the drink Hank wanted, and Hank grew impatient. I said hello and stood beside him. Soon, Billy Martin walked up and joined me. I found myself sandwiched between the Home Run King and the fiery, often-fired New York Yankees manager. Billy and Hank included me in their conversation. Billy had an incredible ability to look straight into my eyes, making it seem like whatever I had to say truly mattered to him. It felt like I was in a Miller Lite commercial —another memorable moment.

Meeting Lefty Gomez Again

Lefty Gomez stopped by the booth to watch the videos and share his thoughts. One thing he said to me was, "I just love those baggy pants." He was kidding, saying the wool pants were darn hot in July.

We discussed the Charles Martin Conlon exhibition at the National Portrait Gallery in October. We enjoyed our visit and agreed to grab a beer and talk about baseball's good old days.

The following day, Lefty stopped at the booth again. We went up to the hotel piano bar, a large, spacious lobby with an escalator leading to the rooms where the executives were meeting. Lefty and I stood at the bar, chatting. I mostly listened to his stories. When the executives and owners emerged from the meeting, they took the escalator down to our level. Lefty waved several people over and introduced me to George Steinbrenner, Gene Autry, and others. That was exciting.

Lefty and I continued our conversation and realized we would each be flying home the next day. It was December, with the threat of an ice storm, and Lefty had an early morning flight to San Francisco. He was anxious about missing his flight and wanted to get home to his wife, June. He asked if I wanted to share a cab to the airport and if I minded leaving early. I told him that would be fine, even though my flight was much later than his. I couldn't pass up that opportunity. So, at 5:00 a.m., we hopped into a cab and headed to Houston International Airport. Fortunately, the bad weather never arrived; the roads were clear. We arrived three hours before his flight, and I still had several hours before mine.

Breakfast was in order. Lefty shared stories about traveling around the world after the 1934 baseball season with Babe Ruth, Lou Gehrig, and their wives, Claire and Eleanor. Fourteen All-Stars were set to travel to Japan to play exhibition games, with Babe Ruth as the manager. Lefty recounted, "In Yokohama, there were 50,000 people to greet us. They wanted to see Babe Ruth."

For Lefty and June, the trip was their honeymoon, a year and a half after their wedding. June O'Dea was a Broadway star, and because of Lefty's Yankee career, they hadn't found time to get away. It was a four-month journey. After Japan, they traveled to Shanghai, Hong Kong, Manila, India, Italy, France, Germany, and the United Kingdom.

He talked about how, as a pitcher, he was a terrible hitter and how Babe Ruth made him a $50 bet that he wouldn't get three hits all season. He said he got two hits in the first game and none for the rest of the season. I looked up the stats, and that's not true, but he was a storyteller and a funny guy.

In another story, he said the only bat he ever broke was his grandson's, which he accidentally ran over while backing out of the garage.

Lefty talked about his feelings on May 2, 1939—a historic day. In Briggs Stadium in Detroit, Michigan, after 2,130 consecutive games, Lou Gehrig, "the Iron Man of baseball," removed himself from the lineup. Lefty said it was an emotional time for Lou and his teammates. The Detroit fans gave a thunderous ovation, and Lou began to weep. The players in the dugout were stunned. I have a photo of Lefty sitting on the top step near Lou. Lefty looks like he doesn't know how to break the ice. Should they talk to Lou or leave him alone? Lefty said he would never forget that moment. He was sitting next to Lou on the dugout step, and after the applause subsided, he said, "Hell, Lou, it took fifteen years to get you out of there. Sometimes, I'm out in fifteen minutes." Lefty broke the ice, and Lou laughed. This was all new to me. I kept asking questions and hearing about George M. Cohan, Ernest Hemingway, Jack Dempsey, George Gershwin, James Michener (he wanted to write a biography of Lefty), Fidel Castro, and many famous baseball players. It was great; Lefty spoke, and I listened. He had a million stories to tell me.

I asked him if he knew Joe DiMaggio well. I had no idea they were so close. He could have talked for hours about Joe. He said, "We both came from the San Francisco Bay Area. I had been with the Yankees for six years, and we were roommates for the next seven years. I helped chaperone Joe because he was very young and unsure about being in a city like New York, which made us close friends." He told me that in the 1950s, he often dined with Joe, Marilyn Monroe, and June, and that the wives would discuss show business for hours. Lefty also said that he and Joe attended an old-timers game, where Joe mentioned that he and Marilyn planned to get married again on August 8, 1962, and wanted Lefty and June to attend. Sadly, Marilyn Monroe died four days before that date. The coroner suggested it was probably suicide, but Lefty couldn't believe it because Joe told him they were happy to be together again and that he would support her, in contrast to the reality of their first marriage, where Joe had been controlling. Over the years, Joe and Lefty remained close friends. I was overwhelmed by this information and wished I were better prepared to ask more questions.

As our breakfast ended, he commented on how much he enjoyed the baseball newsreels and invited me to visit his home in California to see his memorabilia and spend more time together. That was exciting; I wanted to make a biographical video of Lefty. However, earning a living got in the way, so I never took that trip. In December 1989, while driving to my office in Washington, DC, I heard on the radio that "Hall of Fame pitcher Lefty Gomez has died." That was sad. I regret not taking him up on his offer.

I needed to learn more about his career, so I researched it when I got home from Houston. I was impressed to discover that he was the American League starting pitcher in the first three All-Star Games beginning in 1933, achieved six World Series wins without a loss, and secured five World Series titles with the Yankees. He also won two Triple Crowns, meaning he led the league in wins and strikeouts and had the lowest ERA in the American League.

I had listened a lot, but I shared one of my stories, about Mickey Cochrane. Lefty thought it was hilarious and stated without a doubt, Mickey Cochrane was the best catcher in the American League, always tough to get out. Below is the story I told Lefty.

First Autograph

My first autograph came from a Hall of Famer. Gordon "Mickey" Cochrane is regarded as one of the greatest catchers of all time. He holds the record for the–highest career batting average among major league catchers with at least 5,000 at-bats, finishing his career with a .320 average. In 1999, *The Sporting News* (TSN) ranked him 65th on its list of Greatest Baseball Players.

In 1931, when Elvin Mantle had a son, he named him after his favorite baseball player. His son was Mickey Mantle.

On a Saturday afternoon in 1957, my father took me to the Lather Brothers garage in West Lake Forest, Illinois. After standing around for an hour and listening to him talk about hunting and the old days, we headed across Waukegan Road to Smitty's Tavern. My father, who was born and raised in Lake County, seemed to know everyone. As a kid, these long conversations seemed endless. Maybe that's where I learned to listen to others and be patient.

It was no different at Smitty's that day, and I sat patiently with a bottle of Nehi orange soda. What was different, though, was that when we got into our 1950 Plymouth Deluxe and started home, my father asked, "Do you know who the guy I was talking to was?"

How would I know? I said I did not. He said, "Well, that was Mickey Cochrane. He was a baseball player. He is in the Baseball Hall of Fame."

Suddenly, I became interested and had several questions. First, what is the Hall of Fame? Second, what did he do to get there? My dad had only a few answers, so I was now on a mission.

Research… I was in sixth grade at a two-room grammar school far from those barstools. The school library had a single bookcase that was three feet wide and five feet high. I searched, but I couldn't find any books about great baseball players among those four shelves. My next opportunity was the big green bookmobile that came to school twice a month. I had no luck again. I asked the librarian if there was a book about baseball's great players. She said she wasn't aware of one but would see what she could find.

After two weeks of waiting, the bookmobile was back. I stepped up to the desk and was welcomed by a big smile and a green book called "Baseball's Hall of Fame." Now, I would find out about Mickey and why he is in the Hall of Fame.

At a glance, the list of Hall of Fame members was impressive. With my limited knowledge of baseball history, I recognized many names: Ty Cobb, Babe Ruth, Lou Gehrig, Christy Mathewson, and Mickey Cochrane. Although each player appeared on only four pages, this was "gold" to me.

I read those pages multiple times and memorized Mickey's statistics: a lifetime batting average of .320, having played on the Philadelphia Athletics' World Championship teams in 1929 and 1930, and being voted the American League's Most Valuable Player in 1928 and 1934. As a player-manager, he led the Detroit Tigers to the World Series Championship in 1935. At that moment, I realized Cochrane was one of the best.

The most alarming part for me was learning about the end of his baseball career. On May 25, 1937, Cochrane was hit in the head by a pitch from Yankees pitcher Bump Hadley (no batting helmets at that time; they became mandatory in December 1970). He was hospitalized for seven days, and his life nearly ended. His baseball career, however, did. At the age of 34, Cochrane was forced to retire after doctors ordered him not to play baseball again. This served as my introduction to the history of baseball.

With this new information, my question was: "Dad, when are we heading back to see the Lather brothers? I have a baseball I want to get signed." Soon after, I enjoyed my Nehi orange soda at Smitty's and got a baseball autographed by a Hall of Fame member.

Unfortunately, I valued the signature on my ball so much that I wanted to protect and preserve it. I decided to cover it with clear fingernail polish. This turned out to be a terrible idea. Later, I discovered there were better methods. Nevertheless, I still have the ball 68 years later.

A Visit to The Sporting News

The Sporting News (TSN), first published in 1886, earned the nickname "the Bible of Baseball" for decades.

In 1987, I worked at the National Association of Counties and spoke at a conference in Jefferson City, Missouri. Since my flights were in and out of St. Louis's Lindbergh Field, I arranged to visit Paul McFarlane at TSN. I had met him a few years earlier at the National Portrait Gallery. He was a former editor of TSN who later became the newspaper's historian, overseeing all of its baseball archives.

Paul's office was on the first floor. I finally reached it after navigating around the editorial staff in a spacious open bullpen and squeezing past a large model of Fenway Park. Paul grew up in a family connected to the Red Sox. *The Sporting News* celebrated its 100th anniversary in 1986, and Paul's office contained a century's worth of history. Stacks of books, letters, newspapers, coffee mugs, quotes on the walls, and a standard typewriter filled the space. 'Cluttered' would be a generous description.

Quotes on the walls:

"How old would you be if you didn't know how old you were?"

"Age is a question of mind over matter; if you don't mind, it doesn't matter." Satchel Paige had borrowed this from Mark Twain.

There was an enthusiastic welcome. I was in the inner sanctum of baseball history. I didn't have a plan; I just wanted to visit this baseball shrine. One intriguing feature in Paul's office was the old bank vault, where he kept the treasures of the past 100 years. He opened the vault using the combination 4-0-6—Ted Williams's batting average in 1941, when he was the last man to hit over .400.

Paul showed me letters and documents from the earliest days of professional baseball, including correspondence from Ty Cobb and others. Additionally, there were books from the game's inception, including *The Base Ball Player's Pocket Companion* (1859) and *Beadle's Guides* (1871).

Contract cards (similar to index cards) filled several cabinets. There was a card for every person who had played in the major or minor leagues. Each card recorded the ballplayer's primary demographic data and contract status. The cards, maintained for over 100 years, dated back to 1886. Although these cards were no longer needed, over 172,000 remained.

Paul was thrilled about "*Baseball in the News*" and had many fascinating stories, but I had to catch a flight.

Hank Greenberg

Hank Greenberg was a Hall of Fame baseball player, a five-time All-Star, a two-time American League Most Valuable Player (MVP), and a two-time World Series Champion with the Tigers in 1935 and 1945. His number "5" was retired by the Detroit Tigers.

He was the first Jewish superstar in American team sports, facing a dilemma during the 1934 pennant race: whether to play baseball during the Jewish High Holy Days. After consulting his rabbi, he chose to play on Rosh Hashanah but sat out Yom Kippur, instead spending the day at the synagogue. Having endured his share of antisemitic abuse throughout his career, Greenberg was one of the few opposing players who publicly welcomed African-American player Jackie Robinson to the major leagues in 1947.

While researching newsreels at the National Archives, I came across extraordinary footage of Hank Greenberg's induction into the US Army on May 7, 1941, seven months before Pearl Harbor. Hank was one of the first Major League ballplayers to volunteer for the US Army. Notably, there were other newsreels featuring Hank in the 1930s and in 1945, 1946, and 1947, when he returned to baseball after World War II. These newsreels predate the advent of television sports reruns, making them a unique and valuable historical resource.

The players I spoke to were amazed to see themselves in action through these newsreels. I was sure that Hank would appreciate this rare footage, so I wrote to him to see if he would be interested in receiving a tape of his playing days. He was thrilled at the possibility of having the old newsreels on videotape. I carefully edited the footage I found that featured Hank and created a special video for him. However, I was unsure whether he used Beta or VHS tapes.

After exchanging letters, I found out that he used a Betamax machine. I promptly sent him the tape.

Hank was most appreciative. He responded, "Needless to say, it brought back many fond memories of friends, places, and events that I had long ago forgotten. I shall cherish the tape and can't thank you enough for sending it."

Later, while reading his biography, I discovered that the time he received the tape coincided with his cancer diagnosis. I hoped the video brought him happiness. Tragically, he passed away in September 1986 at the age of 75.

Yogi Berra

Yogi Berra was a New York Yankees catcher, elected to the Baseball Hall of Fame in 1972. In later years, he managed both the New York Yankees and the New York Mets, leading each to a League Championship Series title.

In 1985, Trish and I sold our three-volume video series, *Baseball in the News*, at a baseball collectibles show in York, PA. Many veteran ballplayers charged for autographs, as the average Major League Baseball (MLB) salary was around $13,500 in the 1950s. This salary was undoubtedly higher than that of the average American worker, but it was still far below the MLB average in 1985, which was over $370,000.

Yogi Berra was signing photographs and baseballs. The first volume of *Baseball in the News*, covering 1951-1955, featured Yogi in many segments. I thought he would enjoy having a video cassette of his playing days, especially since this was before ESPN and the nightly reruns of every play. When I approached his table, I spoke to one of the event staff and explained what I wanted to do for Yogi, and he was happy to escort me to Yogi at the signing table.

I told Yogi I wanted to give him a video cassette highlighting his playing days from 1951 to 1955. He was delighted. I asked him if he needed VHS or Beta format, which stumped him. He was not aware of the type of video machine he owned. I said, "No problem. I'll bring over both, and you can decide."

I returned and showed him the two formats. He was uncertain but said, "When Carmen and I go to the video store on Saturday night, I think we get the small one." So, he chose Beta. I should have given him both formats. What was I thinking? I hope he enjoyed it.

Tony Kubek

Tony Kubek was a shortstop for the New York Yankees from 1957 to 1965. He was the American League Rookie of the Year in 1957, a three-time World Series Champion, and a four-time All-Star.

In the 1970s and 1980s, there were no 24-hour sports channels. The main baseball broadcast option was NBC's Game of the Week. Tony started with NBC in 1969 and served as the voice of the Game of the Week until its end in 1989. His co-hosts during that period included Curt Gowdy, Joe Garagiola, and Bob Costas. Tony received the Baseball Hall of Fame's Ford C. Frick Award in 2009. This award is given annually to one baseball broadcaster for their significant contributions to the game. He had over thirty years of experience announcing Major League Baseball.

On a Saturday morning in January 1985, I called Tony at his home in Appleton, Wisconsin, to discuss the baseball newsreel videos I was producing. I asked if he would consider endorsing my project, and he expressed great interest and encouragement. I promised to send a videotape of Volume I right away. Although he would be in New York for a week, he mentioned that he would review it upon his return.

I didn't want to bother him, so I waited a few weeks and called again on Saturday morning. He apologized for not watching the video and promised to review it by next Saturday.

My next call was interesting. He once again admitted that he hadn't watched the video and said he would watch it that day when his son came home from basketball practice so that he could set up the VCR. A major TV personality at NBC relied on his teenage son to operate the VCR, much like many Americans did in 1985. Tony was very generous in helping me.

I quickly received the endorsement I had been hoping for:

> *"Every nostalgia buff and purist should have Jerry McNeil's video cassettes of 50s and 60s baseball highlights. This is real baseball -- without the DH."*

George H. W. Bush

On a sunny afternoon in 1988, I attended a job-training recognition ceremony in the White House Rose Garden, hosted by George H. W. Bush, the 41st President. The featured speakers included the President and Secretary of Labor, Elizabeth Dole. After the program, I shook hands with the President.

There was no time to discuss our favorite sport, baseball. Bush was a player, a fan, and an admirer of my video series, *Baseball in the News*.

Bush was an outstanding athlete at Yale University. He played first base and served as the captain of the team that played in the first two sanctioned College Baseball World Series in 1947 and 1948.

Rod Dedeaux, the University of California coach whose team won the 1947 series, said of Bush: "He was an excellent fielder and a tough out. I'd put him on my all-time opponent team…"

In April 1947, two young athletes who would later become influential figures in American society met at Yale Field. Vin Scully was an outfielder for the Fordham University baseball team. Scully and Bush faced off in a college baseball game. According to the story, they both went hitless in three at-bats, and Yale emerged victorious, 3-1. Decades later, this event often inspired friendly banter between the two on the golf course.

On June 5, 1948, George Bush, as captain of the Yale Bulldogs baseball team, had the honor of meeting a cancer-stricken Babe Ruth. Ruth was donating an original manuscript of his autobiography, *The Babe Ruth Story*, to the Yale University Library. He presented the gift during an on-field ceremony at Yale Field. George Bush later recalled, "I was the captain of the ball club, so I got to receive him there. He was dying. He was hoarse and could hardly talk. He croaked when they set up the mike by the pitcher's mound. It was tragic. He was hollow. His whole great shape was gaunt and hollowed out." Ruth died on August 16, 1948, just two months after the event.

Years later, when George H. W. Bush served as Vice President of the United States, Craig Fuller was his Chief of Staff. In June 1984, Trish and I got married in Alexandria, Virginia. Craig and his wife, Karen, who Trish knew from work, were longtime friends and joined us in celebration. Craig wanted an update on our video project, *Baseball in the News.* I told him I had completed Volume One, and Volumes Two and Three were in production. Craig said, "The Vice President is going on vacation; he's a big baseball fan and would enjoy the baseball newsreels. How can I get him one for his trip?" I found the idea exciting. The Vice President's office was to contact me about the delivery. A few days later, I received a call asking me to send the tape to the Vice President's office in the Old Executive Office Building in Washington, D.C. I asked if they needed VHS or Beta. The VP would watch the video on Air Force One, but since no one knew the required format, they said they would get back to me. Once they had an answer about the format, time was short, so they told me that someone would pick up the VHS tape in the afternoon.

I had an office in the back part of our home in Alexandria. I got the tape ready for pickup. Early in the afternoon, I received another call from the person picking up the video: "We stopped by to pick up the tape; however, no one answered the door." I was embarrassed to have missed the pickup. I was disappointed that the VP wouldn't have the baseball newsreels to enjoy on Air Force One, but I hoped it wasn't too late. I told them I was home and had the tape ready, in case they could come by again. They responded by saying, "Oh, that's no problem. We're in the car right outside your house." It was 1984, and this was the first time I received a call from a car waiting on the street. I had only seen that on TV.

I told him to come to the door. I hurried through the house, opened the door, and there he was. He handed me a $39.95 check, took the tape, thanked me, and was on his way.

My intention was for the tape to be a gift. However, I didn't object; upon examining the check, I saw it was issued from the President of the Senate's account (the Vice President also serves as the President of the Senate). Pretty cool! I wish I had just kept the check, like saving the first dollar bill a business earns. Unfortunately, we needed the $39.95 more than we needed a keepsake.

A few weeks later, I received a nice photo and message from the Vice President: "To Jerry, from one who loves your tapes of real ball players, Thanks, *George Bush.*" In the following weeks, there would be another photo and a message. When Volumes II and III were finished, I delivered those to the Vice President's office at the Old Executive Office Building, part of the White House complex. Getting cleared to enter the complex is like trying to gain access to Fort Knox.

Steve Katish of the Denver Baseball Commission gave me hard-to-get tickets to the Denver Dream game, then in its second year. Patrick and I had a great time meeting the players and getting signatures. The game drew 58,000 fans to Mile High Stadium to see stars like Hank Aaron, Willie Mays, Bob Gibson, and the Yankee Clipper, Joe DiMaggio, play the Denver Bears. The Bears, Denver's minor league team, recruited Vice President Bush to play on their side.

Yale's sixty-year-old former first baseman hit a single to left-center field off Mitt Pappas. His more impressive moment came on defense when Hall of Famer Orlando Cepeda hit a bullet down the first-base line. "I thought it was going to kill the VP," said Sean Coffey, then a military aide to Bush. However, Bush reflexively dove to his left, knocked the ball down, picked it up, and threw out Cepeda. The crowd went wild.

His old glove from his Yale days had made the play. The glove sat in his drawer in the Oval Office throughout his presidential years, always at the ready.

1984, Lefty Gomez gave this to me during breakfast

1984, Paul McFarlane, me and Lefty Gomez

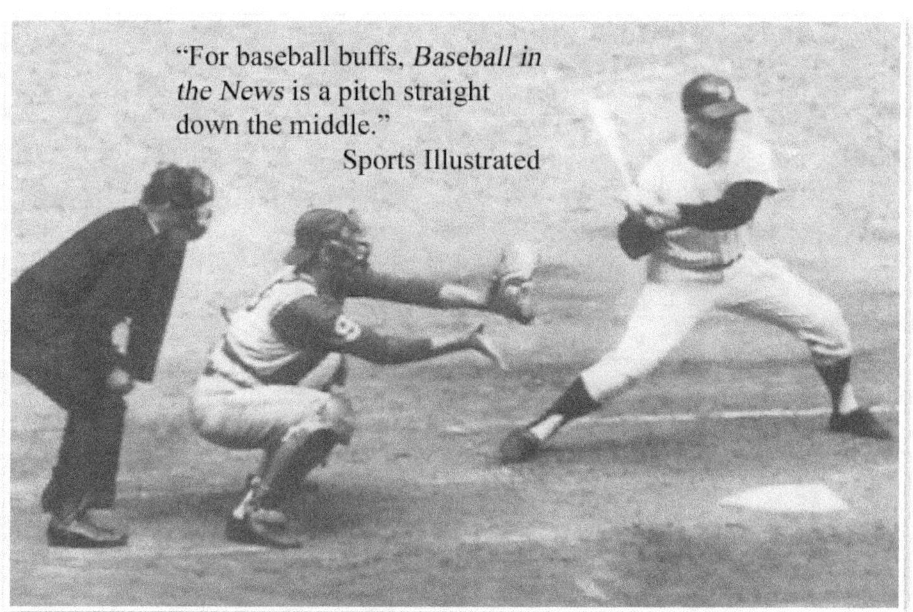

1984, The first *Baseball in the News* promotion card

1985, To Jerry, From one who loves your tapes on *real* ball players-
Thanks, George Bush

April 15, 1985

Dear Jerry:

Thanks for that good letter of April 12 and for my copy of "Baseball in the News". I am sure the whole family will have fun looking at this one.

With warm best wishes,

Sincerely,

George Bush

1985, A thank you from Vice President George H.W. Bush

Hank Greenberg

1129 Miradero Road, Beverly Hills, California 90210

Sept. 24, 1984

Dear Jerry -

Please excuse the delay in thanking you for the tape you so kindly forwarded to me. My Beta Max was being repaired and only recently was I able to review the footage you assembled. Needless to say, it brought back many fond memories of friends, places and events that I had long ago forgotten.

Hank Greenberg -2-

1129 Miradero Road, Beverly Hills, California 90210

I shall cherish the tape and can't thank you enough for sending it.

I shall be happy to review your tape of 1951 to 1956 and give you my comments and testimonial.

Looking forward to hearing from you.

Cordially,

Hank

1984, A thank-you note from Hank Greenberg.

September 24, 1984

Dear Jerry,

Please excuse the delay in thanking you for the tape you so kindly forwarded to me. My Betamax was being repaired, and I was only recently able to review the footage you assembled. Needless to say, it brought back many fond memories of friends, places, and events that I had long ago forgotten.

I shall cherish the tape and can't thank you enough for sending it.

I shall be happy to review your tape of 1951-1956 and give you my comments and a testimonial.

Looking forward to hearing from you.

Cordially,

Hank

1984, Hank Greenberg's Biography showcasing his playing days.

Chapter 18: Outdoor Adventures

At 49, I began climbing mountains. I had been running for years, but after the 1976 Fiesta Bowl Marathon in Scottsdale, Arizona, I developed severe hip and back issues that prevented me from running again. At thirty, my long-standing physical activity came to an end.

2002, With Trish on the summit of Mt Elbert, the highest peak in Colorado

For the next nineteen years, my activities were limited to hiking in the Shenandoah Mountains with Trish and climbing Old Rag. Then, in 1995, I attempted to climb Longs Peak in RMNP. Due to the weather, we turned back from the summit, but I was hooked. This wasn't running, yet it included some aspects of running, such as an improved mood, increased energy, better cardiovascular health, and weight control.

I began considering the mountains I wanted to climb, so I worked hard to improve my fitness. For my fiftieth birthday, Trish gave me the gift of a week of winter glacier training on Mount Rainier. My goal was to climb Denali, so mastering glacier travel was essential.

At our first glacier training group get-together, Lou Whitaker, founder of Rainer Mountaineering, Inc. (RMI), shared some words of wisdom from his extensive experience. Lou was a legend in the climbing world alongside his twin brother, Jim, who was the first American to summit Mt. Everest in 1963. I will never forget Lou's little tip, which I use every time I hit the trail: "If you are not cold when you start, then you are overdressed." This has been good advice.

I spent the week of glacier training learning to use crampons, traveling roped on a glacier, self-arresting with an ice ax (which I would need years later on the Nisqually Glacier on Mt. Rainier), climbing on a fixed rope, and digging a snow cave. Building a snow cave at high altitude is exhausting and wet work, but it provided crucial protection for four of us that week during a blizzard with sixty-mile-per-hour winds.

My next adventure was climbing Mauna Loa, which stands at 13,679 feet, on the Big Island of Hawaii in May 1997—described on the next page, starting at the bottom.

This was followed by climbing Ixtaccihuatl (17,160 feet) and Pico de Orizaba (18,491 feet) in Mexico during November 1997. Orizaba is the third-highest mountain in North America. Climbing to over 18,000 feet was crucial to assess whether I could manage high altitudes. Described on page 187.

In early 1999, I was to be part of a team headed to Aconcagua in Argentina, the highest point in the Western Hemisphere at 22,858 feet. However, the day after Thanksgiving in 1998, two herniated discs set me back—no Aconcagua trip for me next year. Faced with conflicting doctors' recommendations, I tried to tough it out. After six months, I saw a neurologist who told me I needed a discectomy as soon as possible. Before my surgery in May 1999, I couldn't hike and had trouble walking. Trish and I bought a home in Estes Park, Colorado, near RMNP and Longs Peak, which stands at 14,259 feet. While lying in a hospital bed, I resolved to climb Longs Peak before the end of the year, giving me a goal to work toward. Despite struggling with a weak leg and experiencing drop foot, I successfully reached the summit of Longs Peak for the first time in November.

Another discectomy in 2002 improved my leg strength, and I began using an ankle brace. In the spring of 2003, I backpacked in the Grand Staircase-Escalante National Monument in Utah with Jim and Nancy Disney, as well as Jim's son, David, and his wife, Linda. However, in June 2003, I fell while descending the Nisqually Glacier on Mt. Rainier with my son-in-law Richard Floisand. I was able to self-arrest with my ice axe, but it injured my neck. Because of existing osteoarthritis in my neck, I endured severe pain for seven years. My hiking and mountain activities became limited, and I relied on Celebrex to get through each day. When we moved from Estes Park despite struggling with neck pain, I had climbed eleven 14,000-foot peaks in Colorado and seventy-five named peaks in RMNP.

In 2010, after two years working with a chiropractor in Seattle, I was finally able to climb again, although my neck and leg sometimes sidelined me. One of my favorite trips in Washington state is climbing Mt. St. Helens. It's a full-day hike, from 2 a.m. to early afternoon. Although not particularly difficult, the view from the rim of an active volcano is truly unique. I was with Andrew Smiarowski on the first ascent when I was 71. I have done it four times.

I am fortunate to have wonderful friends for hiking and climbing—Doug Day, Paul Pottinger, Andrew Smiarowski, Charlie Eaton, Teresa, and Chris Hagerty—who have always been great partners for exploring the nearby Cascades and a couple of international climbs. We've tackled climbs on Mt. St. Helens, Mt. Baker, and Mt. Adams twice. On our first attempt on Mt. Adams, the conditions were so extreme that Andrew's four-season tent was torn apart. The next year, we made the summit.

With Mount Rainier nearby and its 28 named glaciers, it has become a popular spot for climbers training for the world's tallest peaks. Many of America's top climbers have strong ties to the Seattle area. As someone interested in mountaineering, I have found it both inspiring and educational to meet and learn from some of America's leading climbers of the second half of the 20th century. It feels much like connecting with my boyhood baseball heroes.

I was in Mexico with Phil Ershler, the first American to summit Mt. Everest from the north wall. In Argentina, my team was guided by Craig Van Hoy, who, along with Phil Ershler and Ed Viesturs, was the first American to summit Kangchenjunga, the world's third-highest peak.

Lhakpa Gelu Sherpa was my tentmate in Argentina and holds the record for the fastest verified ascent of Mount Everest from base camp, with a time of 10 hours, 56 minutes, and 46 seconds.

In 2013, Trish and I attended the 50th anniversary celebration of Jim Whittaker's achievement as the first American to summit Mount Everest. Two weeks later, we marked the 50th anniversary of Tom Hornbein and Willi Unsoeld's climb of Mount Everest via the West Ridge. In 1963, Tom and Willi were the first to ascend the West Ridge. It has been climbed only twelve times in 62 years, while Mount Everest has been summited via other routes more than 12,800 times.

In 2018, Tom Hornbein hosted Trish and me for a wonderful visit to his home. As I mentioned before, these climbers and others are like meeting my boyhood baseball heroes.

These climbers offered good advice: "It is always farther, taller, and harder than it looks."

Mauna Loa, Island of Hawaii 1997

Mauna Loa, standing at 13,679 feet above sea level, is the world's largest active volcano (not the highest).

After five days of staffing the Western Association of Counties Conference on Kauai, I left Lihue at 6:30 a.m., flew to Honolulu on Oahu, then to Hilo on the Big Island, and finally drove to Volcanoes National Park. I was unable to obtain a permit to stay in the Red Hill hut, but I did manage to get a permit to sleep on the ground. I arrived at the trailhead at noon. My goal was to reach the Red Hill Hut at 10,000 feet, about eight miles away, before dark.

After climbing 3,400 feet, I reached the hut in four hours and fifteen minutes. On the trail, I met Jean-Baptiste from Grenoble, France, along with Gabriel and Susan from Hungary. I ascended the last three miles with Jean. I slept in a bivy sack behind a small stone wall for wind protection. The scenery was unlike anything I had seen—primarily volcanic rubble. It was a good day, but I started to develop blisters, which I managed to patch. The next day, the route would cover approximately 17 miles. After the sun set, and darkness arrived by 8 p.m. I fell asleep soon after and planned to wake at 5 a.m.

The moon was bright with little wind. However, clouds soon moved in, bringing rain and snow. The night was cold, around 25-30°F. Snow and rain soaked my bivy sack. My sleeping pad, which was under my bivy sack, froze at the exposed end, making my feet cold. Moisture seeped into my sleeping bag. Everything else was stored in plastic bags. I woke up at 5 a.m., made oatmeal, and had coffee. I hit the trail at 6 a.m. Jean Batiste, Susie, and Gabriel caught up by 10 a.m., and I stayed with them for the next two days. The trail was rough.

We reached the crater rim at 1 p.m. and the summit, at 13,671 feet, by 3 p.m. Little did we know that the hike to the summit hut would be the most challenging part of the trip. After retracing our steps for two miles on the west rim, we had to descend 600 vertical feet from the crater rim into the caldera—smooth in some spots but mostly rubble. High winds and unstable footing made it difficult. After climbing out of the caldera, we hiked two miles along the east rim, where loose rocks forced us to go slowly. The worst two miles ever! Susie lost her lunch. Once we reached the hut, we were all completely exhausted. I made mac and cheese and then went to bed. My bag was still wet from last night's moisture, but I didn't care. A park ranger had warned me about the possibility of 70 MPH winds on the summit. The temperature was in the low 30s, and he was right about the strong winds; the hut rattled and shook all night. Luckily, the summit cabin was secured with cables.

The next day, the three of us started the nineteen-mile descent. We began by retracing our steps along a rough two-mile stretch on the east rim. It rained during the second half of our nine-hour journey. The porous pumas weren't slick, so the rain didn't slow us down. I drove to Volcano House in Volcano National Park, where I was so stiff that I had trouble standing upright after getting out of the car. I enjoyed a steak with a view of Kilauea's old caldera. Mark Twain had a similar view when he stayed at the Volcano House in 1866. The iconic Volcano House hotel has been on the rim of Kīlauea in various forms for over 150 years.

Mexico Volcanoes, 1997

Climbing two of North America's tallest peaks in just a few days was an exhausting task. Iztaccihuatl, at 17,160 feet, and Pico de Orizaba, at 18,491 feet, are both located in Mexico. The lead guide was Phil Ershler, the first American to summit Mount Everest from the north side (from Tibet) in 1984. He was also the seventh person to conquer the Seven Summits, the highest peaks on each of the seven continents.

Our team included Phil's wife, Susan Ershler. I recall this was one of her early climbing trips. They eventually reached the summit of Mount Everest on May 16, 2002, becoming the first couple in history to complete the Seven Summits. This remarkable achievement received worldwide media attention, with features on Good Morning America, CNN, The Today Show, The New York Times, and many other outlets. In her highly praised debut book, *Together on Top of the World: The Remarkable Story of the First Couple to Climb the Fabled Seven Summits*, Susan shared her Everest experience. Interestingly, she also included a passage about our days climbing Ixta.

I arrived in Mexico City, which is 7,350 feet above sea level, at midnight. My first day was free until the team meeting at 5 p.m. I took a tour of Teotihuacan, famous for its pyramids, including the Pyramids of the Sun and the Moon. Climbing the Pyramid of the Sun and seeing what was once a city of 125,000 people 2,000 years ago was an exciting experience.

Seeing Ixta from Mexico City was truly breathtaking; its summit was two miles above and looked unclimbable. I had never seen anything so high in the sky. Our first camp was at 12,700 feet. In the early afternoon, we set up our tents and got settled. I was in a three-person tent. With 12 climbers and 3 guides, we would eventually form 3 rope teams.

The next day, we were at High Camp, 14,200 feet. I was sleeping at an elevation that matched my highest summit. We arrived in the early afternoon, set up tents, and melted snow for hot drinks and soup. I filled water bottles, then the weather changed. Snow and wind struck the area as we ate lunch, prompting us to head back to the tents. We couldn't move around to acclimate; instead, we would lie in our sleeping bags.

My mistake was not staying hydrated or eating. The altitude can make it difficult to eat or drink. It was also hard to sleep. When I woke up, the storm had stopped, and Mexico City twinkled below us in the clear air.

At 12:15 a.m., we checked our gear, hydrated, and warmed up. I drank hot chocolate and coffee, ate oatmeal and biscuits, and had a mini Snickers, not realizing it would be nearly my only fuel for the next 30 hours.

At 2 a.m., we hiked across rocky terrain for two hours toward the Ayoloco hut at 15,500 feet. The storm changed our route, and because of avalanche danger, we took a longer route up the glacier. At the glacier's tongue, we put on crampons, and I joined Phil's five-member rope team. The colossal effort was about to start. I positioned myself fourth on the rope. We began the climb and soon crossed steep, ice-covered rocks. I moved over the ice while avoiding the rope. I accidentally stepped on my right boot heel, which caused the crampon to come loose. Although I quickly reattached it, it marked a frustrating start.

It was still dark—about 4 a.m.—and I felt relieved not to see the steep climb ahead. Before we reached the hut, my headlamp stopped working. With the light out, I stayed behind Mario, the local guide, as we crossed snow-covered rocks. We moved quickly across the steep, cold, and tough glacier, barely noticing the climbers' headlamps winding up the glacier below us. At the hut, I drank a third of a quart of water and felt energized. Breathing heavily, I was ready to keep going.

Then daylight arrived, but the sun hadn't reached us, and a cold breeze blew as we paused. The second and third teams were about fifteen minutes behind. Near the top, Phil suggested taking a break to escape the biting wind that would hit us once we crossed the ridge.

Next, we climbed over a snow cornice at the ridge's summit. The sun warmed us, and I felt great. The view was breathtaking. We were now on La Arista del Sol—The Ridge of the Sun.

The pace on the ridge was quick. The summit wasn't much higher, but it was two miles farther away. The break at the top was short. Going down, the weather was perfect. But I was feeling the effects of the altitude. We sat at the top of the Ayoloco Glacier for drinks and snacks. I felt so nauseated that I could barely eat and could hardly drink. We descended to our high camp and packed up. We loaded our 50-pound packs and moved toward base camp. We rested at 13,500 feet, and I was exhausted, still unable to eat or drink. I remember wanting to lie down and groan, but I had to shoulder the pack and descend. When we reached base camp at 12,700 feet, I still felt terrible with a headache and nausea. I was too nauseated to drink or take Imitrex for the headache, so I stayed in the tent, feeling miserable. Others enjoyed stew and hot drinks outside, while I lay in my sleeping bag, feeling worse as visitors asked if I wanted anything. I longed for instant chicken soup, but knew I couldn't keep it down, and the night felt endless.

I woke up at 5:30 a.m., my stomach had settled a bit, and I took two Imitrex. The medication eased my headache, so I went for a walk. Phil was up and walked with me, expressing his relief that I had improved overnight. About an hour after taking Imitrex, I was able to eat and drink. Soon after, Dr. Geraldo Reyes, the owner of the local climbing support team, and another driver came to take us back to town. At 6 p.m., we had dinner at the Reyes home, which made for a pleasant evening, followed by a long sleep in a bunk bed. The air was chilly, but the sleeping bag kept me warm.

The following night was spent at a hotel in Puebla before heading to the village of Tlachichuca. In town, we stayed at a former soap factory that had been turned into a climbers' hostel—a walled courtyard with dorms, a cold shower, and plenty of sunshine. After breakfast, we wandered around town, often looking east at Pico de Orizaba, 18,491 feet tall. I wondered if it would be as nauseating as Ixta. We visited the local indoor market, an authentic spot. Items for sale included hanging meat and poultry. Someone was cooking in a large cauldron over a charcoal fire; the contents were bubbling and looked unappetizing.

We went back to the compound for lunch. Señora Reyes and her daughter had set up a buffet in the dorm. It was a beautiful display. However, one item I couldn't identify but looked like something from the market's cauldron. I decided to play it safe.

After lunch, we got ready to head to the Piedra Grande hut on Orizaba. The 40-year-old Dodge Power Wagon provided a rough ride; we had to stop often because it kept overheating, so we poured water over the radiator. We carried eight one-gallon jugs and occasionally stopped at streams to refill them. We reached our destination late in the afternoon, where small climbing teams from Germany and Italy were already at the hut.

As darkness fell, we ate an early dinner and settled into our sleeping bags, expecting a midnight wake-up call. I quickly drifted off to sleep, but at 11 p.m., I woke up to mice scurrying around the hut — it was a little creepy! I lay there, wondering whether I could summit the third-highest mountain in North America. Still, I was better hydrated and acclimated than I had been two days earlier.

As midnight approached, I quickly put on my boots, packed my gear, and drank coffee and cocoa while eating oatmeal. One team member stayed behind, suffering from nausea. That seemed like a wise decision considering how sick I had felt a few days earlier. I soon set out with the team under a starry sky.

The first 1,000 feet were on rock. We paused at 16,000 feet to put on crampons, eat, and drink. It was freezing then. I was determined not to repeat my previous mountain disaster, so I ate and drank plenty of food and water. I carried two liters of flat Coke, two liters of Gatorade, and one liter of water (a total of eleven pounds).

It was still dark as we ascended an ice gully toward the Jampa Glacier, with the headlamps of the Italian and German teams visible above us. Occasionally, ice fell from above as we climbed. When we reached the glacier, dawn arrived. The views behind us were vast, but ahead loomed the steep glacier.

After ascending the glacier, we reached the volcano's crater rim at 18,000 feet by noon. We set down our packs and, after resting, climbed the final 500 vertical feet to the summit. One member was affected by altitude and passed out; a guide used a short rope to help him descend to a lower altitude.

Reaching the summit was incredible. The crater was huge and unsettling. We took pictures and explored the area. From the summit, we could see volcanoes in the distance. The descent was manageable. We paused at 16,500 feet. I was exhausted and out of water, but a kind person gave me half a liter. It helped me reach the hut. Still tired but not depleted, I was on my feet. Packing up and heading back in the Power Wagons felt satisfying.

We loaded the Power Wagons and headed down the mountain, stopping for a picnic before heading back to Tlachichuca. It was a chilly night, but I was smiling as I lay in my sleeping bag on the top bunk of the climbers' dorm. I had reached 18,491 feet, which was a fantastic achievement. I was 51 years old, and 21 years later, I reached over 22,000feet in the Andes. That was fantastic too.

Ruth Glacier, Denali, Alaska, 1998

After a long day at the NACo office, I flew to Anchorage, Alaska, with stops in Detroit and delays in Seattle. I arrived late at night, took a shuttle to the Best Western Motel, but had trouble sleeping. After a short rest, I caught a shuttle for the 114-mile trip to Talkeetna, arriving about two in the afternoon. I stayed at the Fairview Inn, a small tavern with five rooms on the second floor, popular among climbers.

Staying at such a historic location was a wonderful experience. My room was number five, and it felt like a shrine to Ray "the pirate" Genet. Every wall displayed photos, newspaper headlines, and articles about the famous climber. He was one of three climbers to first summit Denali in winter back in 1968, an achievement that served as the basis for the book *Minus 148 Degrees*.

Although I was tired and wanted to sleep, I spent a lot of time reading about Ray's adventures and his death on Mt. Everest in 1978. One newspaper article had a photo of Ray with his wife, Kathy, and their six-month-old son, Taras, as he left for Nepal. It was all interesting, but I needed to get some sleep.

I woke up early and wandered down Main Street, carrying my duffel filled with gear toward the Roadhouse, known for serving the best breakfast in town. After that, I continued to the Alaska Mountaineering School, a simple building on an open lot.

Colby Coombs, the director, mingled with fellow climbers during check-in. By late morning, all participants had arrived. We enjoyed sandwiches for lunch and then gathered for an overview of the upcoming week. I didn't know Colby, but hearing that he was about to be on the cover of Reader's Digest made me curious. Rumor had it that he had been in a terrible climbing accident and that his climbing partners had died. We didn't want to pry or reopen a tragic memory for him, so we did not discuss it.

In the afternoon, we focused on gear checks, instruction on ropes and jumars, and team assignments. We then finished the evening by setting up our team tents and sleeping in the open lot.

Each team had three members. My tent mates included Roger, an attorney from Dallas, and a twenty-year-old named Taras Genet. Yes! The same Taras I read about at the Fairview Inn the night before. The son of Ray "the pirate" Genet was my tentmate. That was mind-boggling. In 1991, seven years earlier, Taras became the youngest person ever to summit Denali at age twelve.

We traveled to Ruth Glacier in a single-engine plane piloted by Buck, the owner of Spotted Dog Aviation. We set up our first camp near the landing site. Each team had two tents: one for sleeping and the other for the kitchen and dining area. We dug out spaces for the kitchen, seating, stoves, and cubbyholes to store melted snow overnight, preventing it from freezing. The tent served as a shelter over our kitchen and dining space and as a protected gathering spot. We unpacked stuff sacks containing our week's food provisions, which had been measured and stored in clear plastic bags without labels.

That night, as I rested in my sleeping bag on a two-inch air mattress atop a glacier, I remembered that two years earlier, getting out of our waterbed had been a struggle. It was a significant change. It was light until midnight, making it hard to sleep. As I lay there, I heard the distant rumbling of an avalanche. At first, it was unsettling, but when I looked outside the tent, I saw that we were in a very safe spot. Still, the sounds of shifting ice and snow take some getting used to.

On the first morning, I was in charge of preparing breakfast, which included hot water, granola, and powdered milk. It seemed simple, but my tent-mates found it too crunchy. I realized I had accidentally grabbed a bag of dried bean soup instead of granola because the food bags weren't labeled, which explained the crunchiness. I was forgiven.

Before we moved our camp down the glacier, we buried food deep in the snow for our return five days later. Then, using sleds and backpacks, each of us carried and pulled a total of 80 pounds. Traveling on the glacier involves significant risks, so we worked in roped teams to prepare for potential encounters with crevasses. When we reached our new campsite, we stayed roped while the guides checked the area for crevasses and placed flags to mark the camp's boundary. Staying within the designated safe zone was crucial.

One evening, while sitting on the snow benches in our dugout kitchen and dining tent, Colby stopped by. We discussed what we had learned and what was coming up over the next few days. Then the conversation shifted to why Colby would be on the cover of the July 1998 Reader's Digest. He openly shared his survival story, being very candid about the climbing accident that claimed the lives of his two partners, Ritt Kellogg and Tom Walter. His story is considered one of the most extraordinary feats of modern mountaineering survival.

The three friends were caught in an avalanche on Mount Foraker in Denali National Park. When Colby regained consciousness, he was hanging from his rope, in pain, and his pack and mittens were missing.

He had been dangling for at least six hours near the top of a rock buttress, with Tom hanging on the other end of the line, supporting him. The rope to Ritt, his longtime best friend, hung limply over the edge.

Tom was dead, his face a snow-covered mask. “It was a blessing in some ways, not seeing his face,” said Colby. “It allowed me to separate myself a bit.” Colby was in bad shape. His ankle and scapula were broken. It was later confirmed that he had fractured vertebrae in his neck. Dazed from a concussion, he scrambled onto a small ledge. Having retrieved Tom’s sleeping bag, he could only wiggle into it halfway and try to sleep.

When he woke up, he saw that the helmet he was still wearing had shattered. He rappelled down to find Ritt dead, tangled in the other rope. Colby spent nearly 36 hours scavenging from his climbing partners' packs for a tent, food, a stove, and fuel. Then, he had to melt snow, cook, and gather the strength to descend. Alone on a technical ice face, he made his way toward the Southeast Ridge, his only escape route. His fractured foot was barely usable, but he kept his focus on the next step.

It took six days of dead ends, frustration, and agonizing pain to descend. The journey was a nightmare of self-arrests. After five days, he reached the Kahiltna Glacier and luckily found the skis he and his partners had left behind at the start of their climb. Now he faced the final dangerous obstacle: crossing the glacier to Base Camp. Using the skis, he dragged his injured foot, crossed the ice field, and finally reached the airstrip shack and its manager, Annie Duquette. Colby ended up spending three months in a wheelchair and another three on crutches. Neither Kellogg's nor Walter’s body was ever found.

I’ve read many survival stories, but hearing Colby share his experience while we sat on the Ruth Glacier in the shadow of Denali was truly unforgettable. Taras, Roger, and I were shaken by the death and near-death of three climbers. Colby was about to lead us on a long trek across the Ruth Glacier, with the same kind of crevasses he described. Luckily, we weren’t dealing with a broken ankle, broken shoulder, or broken neck. We would be roped into teams of five, but that offered no guarantee of safety.

The next day, we started a long hike on the glacier; I was at the back of the last rope team, holding an ice axe ready to self-arrest and watching the person ahead. If anyone fell into a crevasse, we would need to use self-arrest techniques to prevent further injury. It was stressful. After lunch, Colby told me I would be the first on the first rope team back to camp. I had listened carefully when we were instructed on how to avoid crevasses by navigating around depressions and fragile snow bridges. Leading increased my risk of slipping into hidden fissures on the glacier. My heart was pounding faster. I moved steadily, watching for depressions and avoiding them. I felt relieved when we safely returned to our camp within the marked boundary.

Soon after our return, a radio report warned of winds possibly reaching 80 miles per hour heading our way. We spent the afternoon cutting snow blocks to build four-foot walls around our tents for safety. Although the wind did not arrive, we definitely got a workout building the snow walls.

We returned to the camp where the plane dropped us off, planning to fly back to Talkeetna the next day. We woke early to create a runway for the aircraft with snowshoes, but learned the weather was too poor for pickup, so we stayed in our tents. Before heading onto the glacier, we had cached food, and Roger, Taras, and I feasted on it inside our tent, listening to the wind and hoping for better weather overnight.

The next day was clear, and with snowshoes, we quickly stamped the snow to create a runway. The first plane landed at 10 a.m., and I was lucky to be on it. Although safe in Talkeetna, the second plane was delayed. While taking off, a safety signal lit up, prompting the pilot to shut down the engine quickly. This caused the plane's nose to get stuck in the snow, requiring the climbers to disembark and free it by removing all of their equipment, which allowed the tail to settle. The pilot, uneasy about taking off with the safety signal still on, returned alone to Talkeetna. Buck then made a second trip to pick up the rest of our team, who returned after 5 p.m. It was a long day, but everyone was safe and accounted for.

We had a memorable farewell dinner with the entire team and Taras's mother, Kathy. Meeting Taras and his mother was a delight after reading about them while staying at the Fairview Inn. It had been nineteen years since Taras lost his father on Mount Everest.

The next day, after returning to Talkeetna, I attended a two-day meeting of the NACo Coastal Watershed Committee in Seward, hosted by a member of the Kenai Peninsula Borough Assembly.

Following the meeting, I returned to Anchorage to pick up Trish, who had arrived to spend a few days with me in Alaska. One day, Buck from Spotted Dog Aviation took us on a flight near the summit of Denali in a single-engine plane. The weather was clear, offering stunning views of the massive mountain. Clear days are rare, so we felt lucky to get such great views of Denali. Trish was on crutches, and we hesitated when

Buck asked if we wanted to land on the Ruth Glacier. But we finally agreed, landed, and even took a few steps on the glacier where I had been just days earlier. Back in Talkeetna, we stayed in a historic log cabin rented by the widow of Don Sheldon, a well-known pioneering bush pilot. We spent a few days sightseeing in Denali National Park and finished our stay with a fabulous dinner at The Marx Brothers, a famous restaurant in Anchorage.

Bear Lake to Grand Lake, RMNP 2006

RMNP: I left our house in Estes Park at 1:30 a.m. Trish was awake and wished me well. Was I out of my mind? Who would hike to Grand Lake and back in a single day?

At 2 a.m., I started my 38-mile trip from Bear Lake. The initial stretch covered eighteen miles on the North Inlet Trail, and I wasn't sure I could handle it. If I reached Grand Lake but couldn't hike back, I could call Trish, and she could drive over Trail Ridge Road to pick me up. If I felt strong enough, I planned to return via the Tonahutu Trail for twenty miles.

I had been training and planning for the hike all summer, but I was unsure whether it was doable, given that I had just turned 60 in the spring and had my second back surgery five years earlier. I worried about bears and mountain lions during the early mornings and late evenings. After two miles, I felt my pack was too heavy, so I lightened it by hiding a fleece jacket, rain pants, and extra gloves—probably under two pounds—but it felt lighter for the long trek ahead. I concealed my gear among some rocks behind the Emerald Lake overlook sign, hoping to find it when I returned, which would likely be in the dark.

The weather was cool at 42 degrees, but calm. The night was spectacular, with a clear sky, shining stars, and shadows cast by the moon. I felt strong, both mentally and physically, in a good zone. When I reached the summit of Flattop, I had climbed 2,850 feet; however, the temperature dropped by at least ten degrees, and clouds blocked the moon. As morning approached, I was on schedule, so I paused to filter water from Hallett Creek.

I reached Grand Lake in ten hours, feeling confident and without blisters or strained muscles. I had covered eighteen miles, with twenty miles remaining. I got a cell signal, so I let Trish know I would keep hiking and not to worry—everything was fine. It was time for a quick lunch, filtering some water, and putting on dry socks.

The return trip was fantastic. The climb to Flattop, a scenic 4,300-foot ascent, offered chances to see elk, deer, and eagles, creating a peaceful atmosphere. As I moved toward the Continental Divide in the afternoon, I met only two people, who were curious about my hiking plans. Since it was past midday, they worried that I might face lightning storms above the timberline. They were surprised to hear I was heading to Bear Lake, and even more so when I told them I had started there at 2 a.m. One man asked, "How the hell old are you anyway?"

I reached the Flattop summit at 7 p.m. as light snow changed to rain. With sunset expected around 7:30, daylight was nearly gone. During this time, bears and mountain lions might target a lone hiker.

It was already dark when I reached the Emerald Lake overlook, but I quickly gathered my gear and reached my car by 9:35 p.m., soaked by snow and rain on the return trip. I covered 20 miles from Grand Lake to Bear Lake in nine and a half hours, with an elevation gain of 4,300 feet. Overall, I crossed the Continental Divide twice, hiked 38 miles in 19 hours and 25 minutes, and gained a total elevation of 7,150 feet.

I changed into a dry shirt and headed home. Eager to tell Trish every detail, I realized I needed a long nap first. I couldn't have been more satisfied with the adventure.

Aconcagua, Argentina 2011

After being sidelined from major mountains since late 1998, I was finally ready to try another one. The Mexican volcanoes had given me a sense of what high altitude feels like. Aconcagua, the tallest mountain in the Western Hemisphere at 22,838 feet, would be my next challenge. In Mexico, our high camp was at 14,200 feet, but on Aconcagua, it would be at 20,000 feet.

I spent ten years questioning whether I could climb Aconcagua. Can I get in shape for a 22,838-foot mountain? Did I genuinely want to endure sixteen to eighteen nights in a tent, facing snow, cold, and wind? Would neck arthritis with headaches be a dealbreaker? Could I stay motivated for a year and commit to a three-week expedition?

My training was intense. I completed a four-day climbing course on Mount Rainier, but an avalanche prevented me from reaching the summit. I also graduated from the Seattle Mountaineers' six-month Conditioning Hiking Series, which involved long hikes over rugged terrain. Still, I worried that an injury could suddenly end my pursuits.

This expedition occupied my thoughts all year. My training was disrupted over the last two months by an inflamed Achilles tendon, which caused stress and left me feeling unprepared. Finally, after all the planning, training, and worry, January 8, 2011, arrived. My flights from Seattle to Houston to Miami, then to Santiago, Chile, were delayed six hours, causing me to miss my connecting flight to Mendoza, Argentina. After 33 hours of travel, I reached Mendoza, where I spent the next day doing a gear check and obtaining climbing permits. The following day, we departed for Penitentes and then headed to the trailhead on the Rio Vacas.

It took three days of trekking to reach Plaza Argentina base camp at 13,750 feet. After the 30-mile approach, we had a day to relax and acclimate. I also enjoyed a twenty-peso ($5) Coke. After the rest day, we carried some of our equipment to Camp One at 15,500 feet and secured it under rocks so the ravens could not access it. Then we returned to base camp. A week after leaving Seattle, I made a three-minute satellite phone call to Trish for $15, and she answered. It was great to hear her voice and tell her I was doing fine.

The next day, we carried the remaining equipment and food and spent the night at Camp One. We followed the same process for all three higher camps.

After our night at Camp 1, we carried supplies to Camp 2 at 17,700 feet, then returned to Camp 1 for the night. The next morning, my tentmate Jim was feeling the effects of the altitude and had to leave for home. He went down to base camp and then rode a mule back to the trailhead.

When we reached Camp 2, I got a new tentmate, Lhakpa Gelu Sherpa. Lhakpa was our high-altitude guide and had climbed Everest fourteen times. In 2003, he set the record for the fastest ascent from base camp, completing it in just 10 hours and 58 minutes. By the time I arrived at camp, he had already set up our tent.

Camp 2 was extremely challenging. The high altitude significantly disrupted my sleep, causing me to drift off only to wake suddenly and struggle to breathe. I lay awake telling myself, "I need to stay awake. I don't want to wake up feeling like there's a plastic bag over my head." Still, I would fall asleep again, which triggered another panic attack. This cycle lasted several hours, and my breathing eventually stabilized.

After carrying a load to Camp 2, I strained my neck and developed a severe headache. I used Imatrex, Tylenol, and ice to ease the pain. The ice was convenient because I could get some right outside the tent. I recovered but still experienced some headache issues for several days.

As we climbed higher up the mountain, the days seemed to pass quickly. On the 14th day, we arrived at Camp 3, located at 18,600 feet. By day fifteen, we reached high camp, with the summit attempt scheduled for the next day. However, strong winds and snow prevented us from trying. Spending two nights at 20,000 feet led to restless sleep, and being confined in the tent for 38 hours was not ideal for acclimatization.

Day seventeen turned out to be summit day. I was dressed and ready to go at 3:30 a.m., but I was experiencing balance problems. I was suffering from ataxia and high-altitude sickness, which affected my equilibrium. I talked with Craig Van Hoy, our lead guide, and decided not to jeopardize the other team members. So, it was a big disappointment, but I was in no condition to climb to the summit and return.

I tried to sleep and stay warm when our lead guide, Craig, returned to camp with a team member who started vomiting at 21,000 feet. He was strong and only 28; I was 65. Altitude sickness can affect anyone.

The other five team members summited, but heavy snow and wind hit them during their descent. Mike, one of the team members, was so exhausted that he needed help to descend. Lhakpa carried his pack, and Mike had to support himself with his arm over Lhakpa's shoulder. He should not have been allowed to summit because the conditions were too dangerous. Everyone was safe, but Lhakpa was furious that the junior guide, Matt, had let Mike proceed from the 22,000-foot level when he had been instructed otherwise. My tent mate was hopping mad for a while. Sadly, Matt died in 2014 in an assumed avalanche on Mt. Rainer's Liberty Ridge while leading a group of five other climbers. There were no survivors.

Although I was disappointed, everyone stayed safe. The third night at 20,000 feet was my best sleep in a week. The next morning, we descended 6,000 feet to Plaza de Mulas, a base camp on the mountain's east side. The following day, we faced a 19-mile trek to the trailhead, but due to a sore knee from that day's descent, I chose to take a helicopter along with two others from our group and arrived at the trailhead in fifteen minutes. I showered before dinner, again afterward, and once more the next morning. We enjoyed real food and had a great toilet.

On day 22, my flight arrived at Sea-Tac Airport at 1:30 p.m. after a 29-hour, 30-minute trip. Sweet Trish greeted me with flowers and balloons.

Twenty-two days and thirteen pounds lighter, I was back home. The highlight of our trip was climbing to the higher camps. The most challenging part was packing up and dismantling the camp. The three-day hike to base camp at Plaza Argentina was an incredible adventure.

The uncertainty made each day exciting, and one of the most difficult aspects involved long periods inside the tent at elevations over 18,000 feet. I missed Trish and being able to check in with her.

Mount Kilimanjaro, Tanzania 2013

Kilimanjaro (19,340 feet) was my favorite big mountain climb. It was a seven-day trek that allowed for proper acclimatization. Starting in a rainforest and reaching near glaciers was truly unforgettable. My first night was in Moshi, Tanzania, and walking through the market felt like entering a different world from Seattle.

There were ten climbers on my flight from Amsterdam to Kilimanjaro International Airport in Arusha, Tanzania: three Americans and six Canadians. I was 66; the next youngest was Jean Baptiste, who was 40.

The guide service was Tusker Trails, a top outfit known for its excellent food and medical care, including daily oxygen level checks. Experienced Tanzanians served as our guides. Porters managed the equipment while we carried daily gear, food, and water. When I reached camp, my solo tent was already set up, and my duffel bag was inside.

Upon arriving at each camp, we enjoyed hot water for tea or hot chocolate, along with popcorn and cookies. A delicious dinner wrapped up our day. Saying Jambo, “hello,” became natural, as did “Hakuna matata,” a Swahili phrase meaning "no worries.”

The Lemosho route took seven days, which is two days longer than most climbers take. However, it is the most scenic and provides everyone with a chance to acclimate. The route was 48 miles long and, with all the up-and-down, an elevation gain of about 17,000 feet (more than three miles).

We climbed through the heather, leaving the rainforest behind at around 10,000 feet, and enjoyed the wide-ranging views to the west. At 11,600 feet, the heather gave way to lower shrubs, revealing the Shira Plateau ahead. At this ridge, we got our first view of Kilimanjaro. The hike across the plateau to Camp 2 was short and mostly flat.

The food was excellent. Dinner started with freshly made soup, and we also enjoyed fresh vegetables and fruits brought by the porters each day.

Our third camp, Barranco Camp, was situated at an elevation of 12,950 feet. We began the Great Barranco Wall climb at 8 a.m. on our way to the next camp, Karanga. The dangerous wall had no ropes or safety measures. The Kissing Rock, a narrow ledge on the Barranco Wall, made some people nervous. It can present a big challenge for some, but our group successfully climbed the wall without any issues. We reached the top and entered the alpine desert, which features sparse vegetation and cooler temperatures. Sleet started falling as we approached the Karanga Camp at 13,160 feet.

Not long after I went to bed, I needed to visit the small tented privy. I stepped out of my tent, and the night sky had shifted from cloudy to clear. A bright moon illuminated the mountain, and I saw more stars than I had ever seen before.

As an older team member, I was called "Babu," which means "elder" in Swahili. After a few days, the other climbers wondered why I was the only one with a nickname. When they learned what Babu meant, they all understood. It was the only benefit of being 66. Tanzanians deeply respect their elders, and I felt this respect throughout the climb.

Our fifth camp was Barafu Camp at 15,790 feet. Barafu means 'Ice' in Swahili. When we arrived, we relaxed by taking naps, listening to the sleet, and preparing for an early dinner. At 5 p.m., we had soup and spaghetti with meat sauce. Guide Eliakim reviewed the summit plans and assured us it would be a long day.

Summit Day! We woke up at 4:30 a.m., got dressed, ate breakfast, and left at 5:30 a.m. with our headlamps on. As we climbed above 16,500 feet, the darkness gave way to a beautiful blue sky. We enjoyed watching the sun rise over Mawenzi Peak, one of Kilimanjaro's three volcanic cones.

The hot sun forced us to adjust our layers. The weather became less clear as we reached 17,500 feet, with cold temperatures and overcast skies taking over. At each stop, someone checked our oxygen levels, and several climbers used supplemental oxygen before resuming their ascent. Normal blood oxygen saturation is around 95% or higher. On the mountain, if a reading dropped below 70%, supplemental oxygen was provided. The temperature stayed fairly consistent after crossing 18,000 feet, with a slight increase in wind.

The ascent to Stella Point on the volcano's southern rim, overlooking the crater, was energizing. We saw the Rebmann Glacier at 18,829 feet and had lunch before heading to the summit. At that point, the climb became less steep as we approached the top. We could look down into Reusch Crater, a major depression with small glaciers. Windy conditions persisted. As the Uhuru summit came into view, we hiked along the crater's edge. We reached the peak of Kilimanjaro at 19,340 feet, the Roof of Africa. All ten climbers successfully reached the top.

Celebrations were brief before heading back to Barafu Camp. The scree field was challenging on the knees, but the descent was quick. At 6:30 p.m., we reached camp just before sunset, ending our thirteen-hour trek to the summit. The porters greeted us with hot tea and congratulations. Many were happy that Babu had made it. We enjoyed a warm dinner and a well-earned rest.

The next day, we descended 5,000 feet to Mweka Camp at 10,065 feet. After lunch, we relaxed, sang, and danced. Babu dancing at 10,000 feet brought joy to everyone. Tea was served at 4 p.m., and I enjoyed another peaceful sleep.

On the final day, we hiked to the sign-out station at 5,480 feet after covering a total of 48 miles. Then we headed to Bristol Cottages in Moshi Town, where we enjoyed a cold drink and received certificates commemorating a successful climb.

We had an excellent support team on the mountain, including guides, medical porters, cooks, and extra porters who carry gear, food, and water from the source to the camp each day. Some camps lack nearby water sources, so water must be brought from other locations. Tusker Trails was a first-class guide service. The porters were friendly and helpful, and they also proudly wore the Barack Obama for President buttons I brought. They also appreciated the gum I handed out during the climb.

After completing the climb, I went on a five-day safari to the Ngorongoro Crater and the Serengeti. Staying in a luxury tent in the Serengeti was incredible, with giraffes and zebras outside my tent and the unique nighttime sounds of cicadas, crickets, and bird calls. Each night, we gathered around a campfire after dinner, but had to be escorted back to our tents because of nearby lions. When leaving the Serengeti, the challenge was getting the Thompson Gazelles off the gravel runway so the plane could take off. I wish Trish could have joined me for this part of my trip.

Kilimanjaro was a big success for me.

The Wonderland Trail, Mount Rainier 2014

The 93-mile loop trail around Mount Rainier offered stunning views of the volcano and many of its 28 named glaciers. I camped and hiked near high mountain lakes and glacier-fed rivers flowing through rugged wilderness. I encountered wildlife such as black bears, pikas, marmots, elk, eagles and mountain goats, while the vibrant, abundant high-elevation flowers added color. The Wonderland Trail is breathtaking, mainly because of its 22,000 feet of elevation gain, making the terrain consistently uphill or downhill. The trail was tough—requiring crossings of swollen rivers on log bridges that could be swept away by rain or snowmelt—so monitoring trail and bridge conditions was essential. I divided the hike into seven segments, with Doug Day joining me for four of them. We backpacked the last two. Although the best views of Mount Rainier are hard to pinpoint, my favorite was the northern section, the Sunrise to Carbon River Traverse. This part features high-alpine meadows, the distinctive Burroughs Mountains near Sunrise, the incredible Carbon and Winthrop Glaciers, and the scenic trail connecting the Carbon Glacier, Mystic Lake, and Sunrise. It's about nineteen miles long, with a challenging elevation gain of 5,200 feet. That was a big day. Completing the Wonderland Trail gave me a strong sense of achievement, even though I started in summer 2010 and finished in summer 2014. Many people complete the circuit in ten days, while others take five to fourteen days. I took four years, but I finally finished it.

Everest Base Camp, Nepal 2016

This adventure lasted 28 days, during which I trekked to Everest Base Camp (EBC) at 17,500 feet and climbed Lobuche Peak, reaching nearly 20,000 feet. I was with the International Mountain Guides (IMG) from Ashford, Washington. The trip to Nepal included an overnight stop in Seoul, South Korea, en route to Kathmandu. There, I was first introduced to Teresa and Chris Hagerty, as well as Paul Pottinger, all from Seattle. Traveling alone, it was great to have the support of these three. Teresa and Chris, telecommunications experts, helped me set up a cell phone in Kathmandu that I used to contact Trish most days during the 28-day trip. Paul had been on Everest the previous year when the earthquake struck, and he was stranded at Camp Two for several days. He provided us with excellent advice as we made our way to EBC and during the icy climb of Lobuche.

We started our trip to the Khumbu Valley with a flight on Sati Airlines from Kathmandu to Lukla, often called one of the world's most dangerous airports. There are no roads leading to Lukla. Flying low over the mountains, villages, and terraced fields was incredible. We landed safely to applause. From there, everything up the valley is carried by yaks, mules, and Sherpa porters.

The rest of our group was scheduled to arrive in the afternoon. After lunch, we were about to start hiking when I suddenly started vomiting.

Emily Johnston, MD, a trained wilderness doctor, was our guide, and she diagnosed my problem as food poisoning. She thought it was probably from the welcome dinner the night before in Kathmandu. The team continued while I stayed behind for the night. I stayed at the Paradise Lodge, where a woman named Dawa made sure I was well cared for throughout the night. Our second group arrived late and also spent the night at the Paradise Lodge. The next day, we headed to Phakding. I was weak, which slowed me down; it took several days to recover fully.

The trails often wound along the sides of the mountains, and we had to stay alert. To stay safe, we always stayed on the high side when the yaks passed by because otherwise they might bolt and knock us off the mountain. The yaks carried supplies for the villages up the valley, and on the way down, they were often loaded with potatoes and other produce for market.

The most emotional part of the trip was carrying my brother's ashes to Pangboche to receive a blessing from Lama Geshe. While still in Seattle, I had been communicating with Ang Jangbu Sherpa, IMG's Nepalese partner, about the possibility of having Dan's ashes blessed. He assured me it would be arranged. Someone suggested there might be an issue transporting the ashes. I checked with airlines and the US and Nepal embassies, but I couldn't get a definitive answer. So I double-bagged the ashes in heavy-duty plastic and included the death and cremation certificates. From the moment I arrived, I kept asking Lopsang Sherpa, one of our guides, if there would be any trouble getting Dan's ashes blessed. He kept reassuring me there would be no problem. In Nepal, the atmosphere seemed more relaxed, and Sherpas often say yes to Westerners like me.

From the moment we left Lukla, I carried Dan's ashes in my pack. He was always on my mind with every mile and every day. When we crossed the Hillary Bridge over the Dudh Koshi (Milk River) and started up Namche Hill toward Namche Bazar, tears filled my eyes. I don't know why, then, except that crossing the bridge seemed to symbolize Dan's passing over to a final resting place.

For seven days, I carried the ashes and worried that the blessing might be skipped amid other activities. When I finally knelt before Lama Geshe, received my blessing for protection and good luck, and handed the velvet bag with Dan's ashes to the Lama, I knew it was happening. I thought Lama Geshe would perhaps hold the bag up and offer the blessing, but I was wrong. He wanted access to the ashes, and I had secured the bags so tightly that we could not open them. Someone offered a pocket knife to cut the bag. Now the blessing could begin. While looking at a photo of Dan, he chanted, sprinkled water onto the ashes, tossed seeds into them, and continued chanting as he held the bag aloft. During this time, I was crying, actually sobbing. This was one of the final steps in Dan's passing. That evening, in accordance with Buddhist tradition, I released the ashes into the Dudh Koshi River at Pheriche, marking a profoundly emotional moment during my trip.

It took us ten days to reach Lobuche Camp, an IMG seasonal camp. We stayed in teahouses along the way. Throughout the route, we saw the destruction caused by the earthquake the previous year: collapsed buildings and piles of rubble. My roommate for the trip was Cristiano Mueller from Brazil. In the teahouses, we slept in sleeping bags on plywood platforms. There was no heat, so the nights in the sleeping areas were extremely cold. In the dining areas, some stoves burned yak dung, making the space a bit warmer; however, this also contributed to indoor air pollution.

Additionally, the drinking water came from nearby rivers. Since there was no water treatment, wastewater ended up in the same river, so we always had to filter our water. No brushing teeth with tap water!

We acclimated to the altitude during the days leading up to our arrival at Lobuche Camp at 15,800 feet. This was a good camp; we slept in two-person tents, and there was a cook tent with great staff and a dining tent. We stayed there for two nights, and during that time, it was my 70th birthday. To celebrate a 15,800-foot birthday, I got a pan of warm water, washed my clothes, and then laid them on a large rock while I took a nap. After dinner, our Sherpa team presented me with a delicious birthday cake. Having a cake baked at that altitude was a real gift. I hadn't been that high on my birthday since I turned 21.

From Lobuche Camp, we set out on a long one-day trek to EBC, where we stayed for three nights. This camp is massive, often hosting over 1,000 people, including climbers, hikers, medical staff, porters, and support crew. Surprisingly, there was a small shower tent at our IMG camp. After a couple of weeks, that shower felt fantastic. We explored the base of the Khumbu Icefall, where Everest climbers must navigate massive ice columns and crevasses to reach Camp One. One afternoon, we had the chance to practice our ice-climbing skills in preparation for Lobuche Peak. The nights were cold, around 0 degrees, and the daytime highs reached about 32 degrees. It was truly a once-in-a-lifetime experience. Wow! The 360-degree view was breathtaking.

After leaving the EBC, we returned to Lobuche Camp and then climbed over a thousand feet to set up our camp at 17,000 feet, where we spent a brief night. We started our ascent around 4 a.m. The first part of the climb was on dry rock, followed by large rock slabs where we clipped our harnesses to fixed ropes. Around 18,000 feet, we reached the snow and ice, put on crampons, and began ascending the steep terrain. I was clipped to a fixed rope, which gave me a sense of security. Paul mentioned that the previous year, the entire area was covered in snow, making it easier because kicking steps into snow is safer and requires less effort. For me, at 70, this was significant. I reached the summit, enjoying a breathtaking view of Mt. Everest, Lhotse, Nuptse, and the Khumbu Valley. We took some time to rest, drink, eat, and take photos. Descending was challenging, requiring self-repelling down the icy mountainside, which was difficult for me due to a pre-existing injury to my rotator cuff; when I returned to Seattle, I had rotator cuff surgery. Thanks to the generosity of friends and family, my trip raised over $3,000 for my local food bank, Family Works, supporting their efforts to combat senior hunger.

We descended to Lobuche Camp and said our goodbyes the next morning. The Everest climbers were heading back to EBC to attempt to summit the world's highest mountain. Some members were trekking to a different valley; three people had flown back to Lukla by helicopter due to fatigue and other health reasons.

I was making the three-day, 45-mile return trip to Lukla with a guide, Mingma Sherpa, through Namche Bazaar, the largest commercial hub between Lukla and Everest Base Camp. Mingma wanted to take a slight detour to the village of Dingboche to help a relative with a problem at their teahouse. While he worked, I had the chance to have lunch and watch a man plow an adjacent field with a mule—an unusual sight in our 21st century.

As I reached the final hill leading to Lukla, I stepped onto a stone-covered path lined with yaks loaded with supplies and Sherpa porters carrying loads that seemed impossible to bear. Then, surprisingly, in front of me was Kymber, the president of my Seattle-based food bank, Family Works. She and her family were volunteering in a nearby village and were in Lukla when I was returning from EBC. We had a quick visit, then I went to the Paradise Lodge for rest and dinner, planning to get a good night's sleep before catching a 6 a.m. flight to Kathmandu. I was exhausted and ready to go home.

It was a short walk at 5 a.m. from the lodge to the airport terminal. Unfortunately, bad weather had delayed all flights, so I had to wait. Finally, late in the afternoon, Ang Jangbu Sherpa arranged for me to ride in a helicopter with four other trekkers from Pennsylvania. The helicopter landed a short distance down the hill from the Paradise Lodge on a gravel pad. There were no fuel tanks or pumps—just five-gallon fuel jugs, which were poured into the helicopter's tank. It was a crazy ride. Limited visibility and strong winds made the flight challenging.

The pilot—a former member of the Indian Air Force—struggled to get us over the mountain ranges. From my seat next to him, I watched the altimeter and the mountains ahead, and it was clear we wouldn't reach enough altitude to clear them. The pilot banked right, circled to gain more height, and tried again, repeating this process several times. When we landed, the five passengers cheered enthusiastically and thanked him.

That evening, I enjoyed a hamburger and French fries with my new friends from Pennsylvania. I was so tired; I just wanted to rest, get on a plane to Bangkok, then to Osaka, and then head home. I had a free day before starting that trip. While talking with Trish, I told her how exhausted I was and that I just wanted to rest before heading home. But she rightly encouraged me to explore Kathmandu for the one day I had left.

What a day it turned out to be, starting with The Garden of Dreams in the heart of the noisy, crowded, and polluted city. The site features a neo-classical historic garden, hidden behind stone walls, with pavilions, fountains, gardens, and a remarkable sense of peace. In the afternoon, I hired a Hindu man to give me a half-day tour. I walked alongside cows in the street and visited the 15th-century Hindu Pashupatinath Temple. There, a gentleman who had died that morning on the tennis court was being cremated, and his ashes would later be scattered in the Bagmati River.

Bouddhanath Stupa, a Buddhist temple, is a UNESCO World Heritage Site in Nepal and a significant spiritual landmark. I viewed it from the outside, but due to the earthquake, it was undergoing major repairs.

As I traveled that day, remnants of the previous year's earthquake were still visible as rubble. Wooden beams supported many buildings. Although the structures weren't built to withstand earthquakes, most of them survived. At the Swayambhunath Temple, also called the monkey temple, there was noticeable damage, but the monkey population appeared unaffected. I've never seen a monkey drink Sprite from a bottle before. The monkeys are pretty clever. It was a long day for a tired trekker, but it was entirely worth it.

Weeks after I got home, I found out that Paul and Cristiano had both reached the top of Everest. Cristiano was the fourth Brazilian to do so, and Paul had now summited the highest mountain on each of the seven continents. It was an incredible journey—challenging physically but emotionally rewarding, and it took place in a truly unique part of the world.

My three new friends from Seattle became hiking and climbing partners. Teresa led many climbs of Mt. Adams, Mt. St. Helens, and Mt. Baker, as well as numerous hikes in the Cascades over the years.

Aconcagua, Argentina 2018

This was my second attempt to climb the highest mountain in the Western Hemisphere. The first was in 2011, when I experienced ataxia at high camp and did not reach the summit. On this trip, the guide service I used, Grajales Expeditions, has a long history of providing expeditions to Aconcagua.

I left Seattle for Mendoza, Argentina, on February 16. I built in an extra day to acclimate to the altitude and adjust to the time zone after nearly 24 hours of flying. Unfortunately, my duffel bags didn't connect in Buenos Aires. For two days, I worried they wouldn't arrive. On the third day, they finally showed up. I got a ride to the airport with a Grajales driver to pick up my bags; he was also picking up a contestant trying to summit Aconcagua for a TV reality show. The passenger was very tall, 6'10", and we had a great conversation during the drive back. I later found out he was Fabricio Oberto, an NBA player with the 2007 NBA champion San Antonio Spurs, and a gold medalist for Argentina at the 2004 Olympics. He was a lot of fun to be around, and we connected multiple times on the mountain.

Our climbing team was small, consisting of just five members. I was 71, while the others were in their 30s: Nandhini, a woman from Mumbai, India, and three men — Diego, Juan, and Nicolas — who were friends from Buenos Aires. As we climbed the mountain, I shared a tent with Diego. Our lead guide was Ilan Zeimer, and a second guide, Charley, joined us at Plaza de Mulas base camp.

During the three-day trek to base camp, we stayed at Confluencia Camp at 11,150 ft for two nights and acclimated with a seven-hour hike to Plaza Francia, which offered stunning views of Aconcagua's South

Face. On the way back to Confluencia Camp, I fell and tore the nail on the big toe of my left foot, which was already nerve-damaged.

I thought my trip might be over, but back at camp, I cleaned and bandaged my wound to reduce pain while walking. The next day, we hiked eleven miles with 3,200 feet of elevation gain to Plaza de Mulas Base Camp at 14,500 feet. It was a long day, and my toe was painful. As winter approached in the Southern Hemisphere, the nights grew cold. At base camp, we enjoyed good meals in a dining tent equipped with a table and chairs, but the temperature was always freezing.

On day 8, we climbed Cerro Bonete (16,417 feet). Reaching a summit over 16,000 feet was a good workout. The days passed quickly. As we headed to Camp One at 16,568 feet in Plaza Canada, snow began to fall. Until then, the route to the summit had been dry and clear. Next was Camp Two, at 18,241 feet, called Nido de Cóndores, the condor's nest. At that point, Nandhini couldn't continue. She wasn't feeling sick; she just lacked the energy to go higher. High altitude can drain your energy. I was still feeling strong as we continued up the mountain.

By the time we reached Camp 3, Camp Cólera, our high camp at 19,586 feet, the snow had stopped, but it was still cold and windy.

On summit day, I felt good. We started around 6:00 a.m., and our first goal was the Independencia Hut at 21,000 feet. That went smoothly. We took a break at the hut and then pushed on to stay ahead of the TV group. We were breaking trail, and the TV group was following behind us.

We ascended the Grand Traverse, which gradually climbs to 21,800 feet. The snow was loose and about a foot deep, making footing unstable. Crossing the Grand Traverse on snow and loose rocks without ropes or ice axes—only trekking poles—made self-arrest difficult, and a fall could be dangerous. We reached a resting spot called the cave, from where we could see Plaza de Mulas, 7,000 feet below. Although I was unlikely to fall 7,000 feet, looking down that slope was unsettling.

The cave was a protected area with its tall, vertical walls, so we stopped to rest. I was getting tired, and the snow conditions made it hard to keep going. I kept thinking about having to descend the "Grand Traverse" when I finished, knowing I would be pretty worn out. It was less than 1000 feet to the summit at 22,838 feet.

When we left the cave to start climbing La Canaleta, a narrow trough, Diego, Juan, Nicolas, and Ilan went ahead. I wish I had been with Ilan, who was encouraging and realistic. I was with Charley, who spoke little English. The path was steep, and I took five deep breaths after each step. The unstable rocks beneath the snow made balancing difficult, especially since my left leg was weakened from nerve damage in 1998. I fell several times into the snow, and it wasn't easy to get back up and keep climbing.

Running low on energy at 22,400 feet and concerned about the snow conditions on the Grand Traverse, I chose to turn back with only 400 feet remaining, prioritizing safety. I felt disappointed as I returned to camp, exhausted but safe. When I reached camp, I was so tired I couldn't even remove a crampon because it was too caked with ice from my boot. At 20,000 feet, the air is thin, and I was worn out, so I decided to wait until morning to deal with the boots and crampons, leaving them in the tent's vestibule. I fell asleep by 8:30 p.m., and around 11 p.m., Diego and the others returned from their successful summit attempt after a seventeen-hour day.

My three successful teammates understood my disappointment and were very supportive. They were especially impressed by how I kept up with everyone on the mountain, even on summit day. I nearly made it. I was 71 and twice their age. Juan said, "Jerry, you must be from another planet." I took it as a compliment.

With the end in sight, the next morning we descended 6,000 feet to Plaza de Mulas, where we slept in our small tents. The following day, we hiked nineteen miles to reach the trailhead. Once at Grajales Headquarters, we got ice-cold Coke in glass bottles—so good that I went for a second.

The next day, I realized my lips were severely burned. When I tried to eat a hamburger on a hard roll, biting into it caused so much pain that I started to tear up. I had to cut it into small pieces to eat, feeling like a man without teeth. Soon after, I embarked on a 24-hour journey from Mendoza to Buenos Aires, then to Atlanta, and finally to Seattle, bringing me back home. As I sat at the Buenos Aires airport, I called Trish to let her know I was headed home.

Ecuador 2020

At 73, my next goal was to climb Ecuador's volcanoes. Unfortunately, eight weeks before the trip, I suffered a bulging disc, which greatly limited my training. The twelve-day journey to Ecuador focused on climbing Cayambe (18,996 feet) and Cotopaxi (19,347 feet). This trip was different from other international climbs because we stayed in huts and hacienda lodges the entire time, eliminating the need to sleep on the ground.

This was my first international climb with friends. In 2016, I met Teresa and Chris Hagerty, along with Paul Pottinger, during my trip to Nepal. Since then, I have continued hiking and climbing in the Cascades with them. I also reconnected with Marjorie Clark, a friend from Seattle, and Paul Devaney, whom I met the previous year in London.

We spent several days in Quito, enjoying the local culture, exploring the volcanic scenery, visiting cathedrals and markets, and trying sopa de papa (potato soup, which we had almost daily). We also visited museums and markets in nearby villages outside Quito. Our historic tours included visits to Inca ruins. Additionally, we hiked to a monument that marked the equator at latitude 0. However, a few years after the monument's construction, it was found not to be on the actual equator. Despite this, the hike was enjoyable. Later, we drove to the real equator monument.

Before our attempt on Cayambe, the acclimatization schedule included two mountain hikes: Fuya Fuya (13,986 feet) and Imbabura (15,190 feet). On Cayambe, we formed two rope teams, each with five climbers. At 3 a.m., just a thousand feet from the summit, my nerve-damaged leg caused significant problems, and the pain in my ankle became so intense that it forced me to abandon the climb. After our summit attempt, we descended to the jungle town of Papallacta, where we enjoyed a relaxing soak in the town's famous hot springs.

Our main goal was Cotopaxi, a volcano known for being one of the most scenic in the world. The wind, rain, and snow made it clear that we could really only climb partway up.

With only two days left, I got food poisoning again, similar to what I went through in Lukla, Nepal. It was a terrible night, and the next day was only a little better. Teresa and Paul were my medical support team. That evening, we had our final dinner at our guide Romulo Cardenas's house. I was still recovering from the food poisoning and could only eat boiled potatoes and bread. I happily skipped Ecuador's specialty, guinea pig, spread out on a board and roasted.

Despite these challenges, it was a delightful trip with great companions.

Grand Canyon National Park 2024

In 2014, my hiking partner Doug Day suggested a four-day backpacking trip from the South Rim to the North Rim of the Grand Canyon, with a shuttle back to our car at the South Rim. I emailed him to share my concerns about being too old—68—for such a trek. After waiting ten years for the permits, Doug had a new plan: instead of taking a shuttle back, we would hike back to the South Rim. Now, I would be 78. Doug was fifteen years younger than I was.

All my adventures tend to come with an injury weeks before I leave. The Grand Canyon was no exception. In November 2023, while hiking in the hills around Palm Springs, I strained my left calf muscle. The strain was sudden and so painful I thought a rattlesnake had bitten me. I looked, but there was no snake. I guess the strain was better than being bitten by a snake. It was a big pain descending the Grand Canyon.

I did physical therapy and tried to condition, but my calf kept causing problems. The week before we were to leave, I told Doug I couldn't make the trip. I was afraid I would reach the bottom of the canyon and not be able to hike back out, which would ruin it for both of us. He said he wouldn't go if I didn't, so I decided to give it a try.

I was always concerned about my pack's weight. We planned to camp at Bright Angel Camp for two nights: one after descending from the south rim and another after our descent from the north rim. We planned to have dinner and breakfast twice at Phantom Ranch, which is near Bright Angel Camp by the Colorado River at the canyon's bottom. We also planned to pick up a sack lunch each time we left. This way, I wouldn't need to carry six meals, which would weigh about six pounds or more. However, days before our trip, a water main broke in the canyon, forcing Phantom Ranch to close for several weeks. As a result, I had to carry food for an entire week. Luckily, Doug kindly carried my tent.

The first day involved a seven-mile descent with 5,000 feet of elevation loss. Man, my calf was hurting the entire way. I mean, big pain. I was worried about how bad it might feel the next day. We had a great camp near Bright Angel Creek with a warm night, so I didn't put a fly cover on my tent. The stars were incredible.

The second morning started with a rehydrated breakfast of eggs, sausage, potatoes, and peppers. That day's hike, which was uphill but not too steep, felt much easier. When I reached Cottonwood Camp, I wasn't sure if I could handle the third day's hike to the North Rim. It would be a tough day with a full pack. We had separate tents and secured a permit to camp at Cottonwood for another night if I couldn't continue. When we went to bed, I hadn't decided whether to go to the North Rim. So, when we hit the sack, there was no plan for the next day. I would assess how I felt in the morning and decide then.

At 3:15 a.m., Doug woke me, but we didn't speak. We both got up, ate breakfast, and I was still deciding whether to stay or go. The nighttime hike would be amazing, especially along Bright Angel Creek with its rushing water. It was mostly about keeping momentum and knowing that if the pain became too bad, I could head back to Cottonwood Camp. I packed up, and we headed out without discussing my leg's condition.

It was a perfect night, and after a few hours of hiking in the dark, we started climbing the north wall of the canyon at dawn. Reaching the rim involved 4,200 feet of elevation gain over a six-and-a-half-mile stretch. Although it wasn't the most painful day, it was definitely the toughest. The North Kaibab Trail to the North Rim is the least visited and most difficult of the main routes into the inner canyon. The North Rim stands 1,000 feet higher than the South Rim. About two miles from the North Rim, we passed through the impressive Supai Tunnel, carved through Redwall Sandstone in 1928. By the time we reached the North Rim, there was light snow, and we couldn't find the campsite. There were no signs, and all services were closed for the season in late April. I was exhausted. After finally finding the campsite and setting up, I took a nap while Doug explored. After dinner, feeling cold and tired, I went into my tent and crawled into my sleeping bag.

The next morning was cold, and it took me an hour to get out of my sleeping bag. I had to gradually warm each piece of clothing by pulling it inside the bag one at a time. As we descended, my leg pain was manageable. The last two miles to Cottonwood Camp were marked by steady rain, which forced us to set up our tents in the wet conditions. Doug boiled water, and then I rehydrated my Chicken Alfredo Pasta.

On the fifth night, we returned to Bright Angel Camp, with two more days of hiking to reach the South Rim. Our last night would be at Havasupai Gardens Camp.

Every day was tough on my leg, and I was in pain, but I could handle it. The first day was the hardest, but luckily, I didn't need to be rescued. That's the last thing a seasoned adventurer like me would want.

It was an incredible seven-day adventure covering 60 miles and climbing 10,000 feet. Luckily, it was late April, so the heat was manageable, though we faced some rain and snow. Describing this experience is difficult; it's about witnessing breathtaking sunsets and the changing light on the towering canyon walls of this geological wonder, and much more.

I look forward to doing it again.

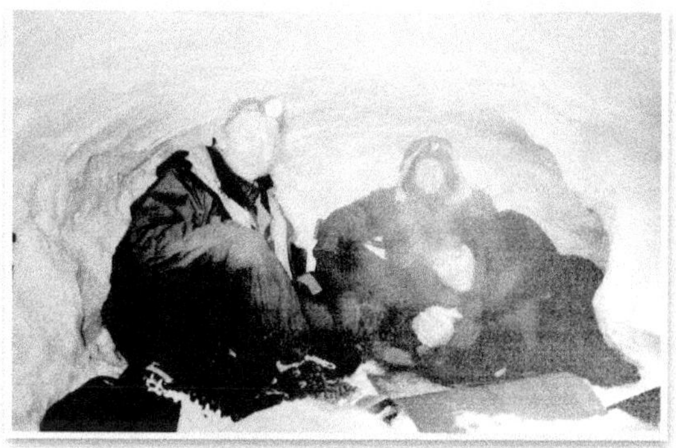

1996, Snow cave on Mt Rainier

1997, Pyramid of the Sun,
Teotihuacan, Mexico

1997, La Arista del Sol- ridge of the sun,
Iztaccihuatl, Mexico

1998, Talkeena, Alaska

1998, Ruth Glacier, Alaska

2011, Aconcagua High Camp, 20,000 feet, Argentina

2013, Kilimanjaro - Big laughs, dancing at 10,000 feet

2013, At the Serengeti Camp, I am known as Babu in Swahili, which means "the elder."

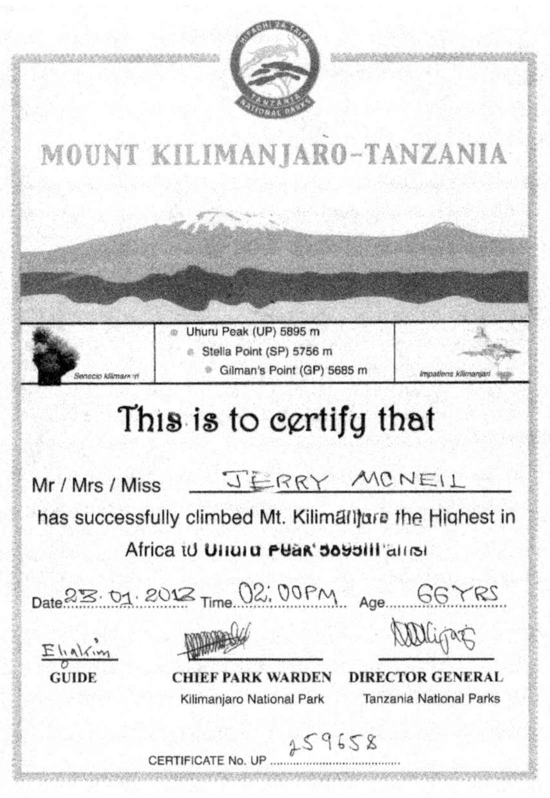

HIFADHI ZA TAIFA
TANZANIA NATIONAL PARKS

MOUNT KILIMANJARO-TANZANIA

Senecio kilimanjari

- Uhuru Peak (UP) 5895 m
- Stella Point (SP) 5756 m
- Gilman's Point (GP) 5685 m

Impatiens kilimanjari

This is to certify that

Mr / Mrs / Miss JERRY MCNEIL

has successfully climbed Mt. Kilimanjaro the Highest in Africa to Uhuru Peak 5895m amsl

Date 23.01.2013 Time 02:00PM Age 66YRS

GUIDE

CHIEF PARK WARDEN
Kilimanjaro National Park

DIRECTOR GENERAL
Tanzania National Parks

CERTIFICATE No. UP 259658

2013, Kilimanjaro Summit Certificate

2013, With Kombe on the Serengeti

2016, While in Lukla, Nepal, Dawa took care of me after
I suffered from food poisoning.

2016, With Lopsang Sherpa and Lakpa Sherpa in front of the
Tenzing Norgay Memorial in Namche Bazaar.

2016, With Paul Pottinger on my 70th Birthday at 15,800 feet in Nepal.
(photo by Teresa Hagerty)

2016, Cristiano Mueller, from Brazil, was my tent mate at Lobuche Camp.

2016, Taking a break on the ice of Lobuche Peak in the Khumbu Valley, Nepal

2016, Ice climbing at Everest Base Camp

2016, Summit Lobuche Peak

2018, Summit of Cerro Bonete, 16, 417 ft, with Aconcagua summit in the background

2018, With Tom Hornbein at his home in Estes Park. In 1963, Tom and Willie Unsoeld were the first climbers to ascend the West Ridge of Mt. Everest.

2024, With Doug Day on a backpacking trip from the South Rim to the North Rim and then back to the South Rim of the Grand Canyon over seven days.

Chapter 19: History Resume Style

Summary of Professional Experience

1971-1974 Employment Counselor
Division of Employment and Training
Colorado Department of Labor and Employment
Alamosa and Colorado Springs, CO

Provided services to clients by assessing their job readiness and skills, screening and referring candidates for Job Corps, and managing referrals under the Manpower Development and Training Act. Offered job counseling and assistance with unemployment insurance claims. Built strong relationships with employers and staff programs such as the Neighborhood Youth Corps, the Work Incentive Program (WIN), and Summer Jobs for Youth.

1974-1976 Assistant Work Incentive Program Coordinator
Division of Employment and Training
Colorado Department of Labor and Employment
Pueblo, CO

Managed funds for programs including Public Service Employment, On-the-Job Training, and Vocational Education Training. Approved contracts, contributed to budget development and implementation, and established policies and procedures for management and operations. Oversaw and evaluated programs across ten field offices. Implemented the Comprehensive Employment and Training Act (CETA) in the state's southern region.

1976-1978 Program Administrator

Western Area CETA Program
Division of Employment and Training
Colorado Department of Labor and Employment
Grand Junction, CO

Directed the operation and evaluation of all Comprehensive Employment and Training Act (CETA) programs across 21 counties in Western Colorado and two Indian Reservations. Managed budgets and personnel functions. Interpreted federal regulations to develop local policies. Created and led staff training initiatives. Supervised Area Office CETA staff directly and oversaw 28 field staff across twelve locations, managing a $5 million budget in FY1978.

1978-1983 Director, Office of Rural Job Training

Colorado Department of Labor and Employment
Denver, Colorado

Managed the CETA program and oversaw its transition to the Job Training Partnership Act (JTPA) across 54 Colorado counties, supervising 45 staff members and an annual budget of $23 million, equivalent to $112 million in 2025. Supervised all operational, programmatic, and fiscal functions and led evaluation and monitoring efforts. Managed a governing board composed of county officials from nine planning regions and private industry members. Served as a liaison and representative for the program office with the General Assembly, the Governor's cabinet, external groups, and the media. Developed and led the Tri-State Consortium for Energy Training for Wyoming, Utah, and Colorado. I served on the Colorado Employment and Training Council by gubernatorial appointment.

1983-1991 Great American Pastimes Company

President and Co-Founder

Alexandria, Virginia

Created a three-part video series called *Baseball in the News: Classic Newsreels*, which gained national recognition and was featured in Sports Illustrated, Sporting News, Good Morning America, the Maury Povich Show, and various video and sports collectible trade publications. Developed product ideas. Managed a sports video catalog. Led marketing, production, and fulfillment operations.

1985-1991 Director, Employment and Training Programs

National Association of Counties

Washington, D.C.

Provided leadership to county officials overseeing federal job training programs. Managed all grants, contracts, and fee-for-service activities related to federal job training. Conducted needs assessments. Offered technical assistance and organized conferences and workshops. Analyzed policies related to federal job training legislation and directives from the executive branch. Supervised membership recruitment, information distribution, and staffing for the Board of Directors of the NACo Employment and Training Administrators (NACETA).

1991-1995 Director, Environmental Programs

National Association of Counties

Washington, D.C.

Founded the Environmental Program in 1991 and expanded it into a unit addressing a broad range of environmental issues with a team of ten staff members. Secured funding and managed all grants, contracts, and membership services related to environmental efforts. Conducted needs assessments, provided technical assistance, and organized conferences and workshops on topics such as radon/indoor air, municipal solid waste, national office paper recycling, coastal watershed protection, source water protection, and pollution prevention.

1995-1997 Director of the Community Services Division
National Association of Counties
Washington, D.C.

Led a team that developed innovative ideas, secured funding, and managed programs and grants focused on environmental issues, housing, transportation, sustainable development, aging, job training, rural development, and intergenerational concerns. Supervised a staff of twenty. Supported county officials and served as a communication link with the federal government. Organized training sessions with county officials nationwide. Partnered with the US Conference of Mayors to create the Joint Center for Sustainable Communities. Established NACo's Smart Growth Initiative to help communities protect the environment and stimulate local economies. Directed the National Association of County Planners, overseeing projects in watershed protection, water quality, pollution prevention, waste management, wetlands conservation, affordable housing, aging services, workforce development, transportation, and volunteerism.

1997-1999 Deputy Director, County Service Department
National Association of Counties
Washington, D.C.

Managed and coordinated activities across five divisions: Community Services, Program Development, Training, Research, and Conferences. Developed a three-year strategic plan and an annual budget, ensured objectives were met, implemented and supervised operational improvements, and improved coordination within and between NACo departments. Represented NACo at various meetings and conferences. Served as the administrator for the Joint Center for Sustainable Communities and acted as a liaison to the President's Council for Sustainable Development.

1999-2001 Environmental Consultant

Western Community Stewardship Forum
National Association of Counties
Estes Park, Colorado

In collaboration with the Sonoran Institute in Tucson, AZ, teams from rural western counties that served as gateways to National Parks or were experiencing rapid population growth were selected. The county teams included elected county commissioners, executives, county planners, and other staff. Conducted workshops and provided technical support for community and county leaders on land use, population management, and sustainable development strategies.

2007-2024 Office Manager

Floisand Studio
Seattle, Washington

Processed payroll, prepared customer invoices, and handled all financial transactions. Managed forms and documentation for new employees. Filed all relevant federal and state quarterly and annual employee tax reports. Drafted employee benefits policies. Submitted incorporation documents and annual reports to the Secretary of State.

Chapter 20: Education

1952-1960 Rondout Grammar School
Rondout, Illinois

1960-1964 Libertyville High School
Libertyville, Illinois

1964-1970 Northern Illinois University
Bachelor of Science in Education
DeKalb, Illinois

1971-1973 Adams State College
Master of Arts in Guidance and Counseling
Alamosa, Colorado

1978 Harvard University
John F. Kennedy School of Government
Institute for Employment and Training Administration
Boston, Massachusetts

Chapter 21: After Thoughts

Now, in my 80th year, sharing these memories has helped me reflect on and reminisce about the special times in my life. Some memories are left out; I can't include everything that has shaped my journey. Some important people are not mentioned. Still, these memories will always stay with me.

My life has had many peaks and valleys. I tend to focus on happier memories and haven't dwelled much on the difficult times. The depression I experienced throughout most of my adult life affected me deeply. I regret not being more present with the children as they grew up. I tried to stay connected, but long-distance communication was difficult, and I often struggled to maintain that bond. Depression has impacted my ability to reach out and communicate.

I feel fortunate to have grown up in the Midwest during the 1950s and 1960s, a time that aligned with America's post-World War II era. My family life was simple but secure. Growing up on that Dusty Road allowed me to mature without pressure or high expectations. It was wonderful to have the independence and freedom to make mistakes and chase my dreams. The two-room grade school may have limited my education in some ways, but it also taught me to build human relationships, develop leadership, and take responsibility. I learned to work with people and accept others, just as I had hoped to be accepted.

Libertyville was a wonderful place to grow up during my teenage years. I had great friends, lots to explore, and many job opportunities.

Taking up long-distance running helped build my confidence, gain acceptance into a large high school, and eventually transition to college. Every time, running helped me secure a spot in the group, allowing me to find my place in a new environment. It also supported my mental health throughout high school and college, and I now see that climbing mountains offers many of the same benefits. Both activities can be meditative and help reduce stress and anxiety. The depression and anxiety I faced were serious challenges, but with Trish's love and support, I persevered for over forty years.

I never excelled academically, but I was fortunate to go to college when it was affordable. Despite difficulties, I managed to graduate and enjoy the many benefits of having a college degree.

As new employment opportunities arose, I took risks. Often lacking specific education or experience for the roles, I quickly learned and adapted. My interpersonal skills proved essential in completing the tasks.

My dreams were often vague, except for my desire to live in Colorado. I seized the opportunities that came my way, turning each one into a stepping stone.

In 1974, I was appointed as an administrator of a program with substantial autonomy to achieve its goals. This independence persisted throughout my career. As a result, I earned my superiors' trust by consistently delivering results. On two occasions, I took charge of organizations facing decline and disarray. Both times, I managed to turn them around, leading to significant improvements and awards for their accomplishments.

Growing up as an outdoor enthusiast, I found solace in hiking and climbing during a time when my mental health required that kind of therapy.

I feel like I’ve experienced an era full of opportunities. My parents had a way of fostering self-responsibility. Although challenges and obstacles have always been around, I’ve consistently found ways to overcome them or change my course. My parents guided and supported me, enabling me to take advantage of opportunities that came my way.

I can't fully thank Trish enough for her unwavering support over the past 40 years. We've helped each other while also chasing our individual goals. We're a great team.

I'm incredibly grateful for all the opportunities I've received.

Chapter 22: Three and Four Generations

This section includes birth, death dates, and marriage information for Mother's and Father's parents, siblings, and their siblings' families.

Seyl - my mother's family

My grandparents, their children and their grandchildren

Joseph Anthony Seyl, 1870-1917 = Julia Alice Carroll, 1876-1941

Joseph Anthony Seyl II, 1901-1962 = Mildred A Krueger, 1907-1973
Phyllis Lita Seyl 1926-1963
Joseph Anthony Seyl III 1930-2013
Michael Martin Seyl 1942-

Harriet Francis Seyl, 1903-1984 = Benjamin L Siljestrom, 1905-1982
Shirley Louise Siljestrom 1925-2002
Jeanne Ann Siljestrom 1927-1984

Eugene Haven Seyl, 1905-1986 = Bertha Marie Hook, 1905-1987
Ronald E Seyl 1932-2021
Barbara Gay Seyl 1934-2012

Lincoln Stephen Seyl, 1907-1949 = Florence Teresa Schmidt, 1912-2001
Stephen Joseph Seyl Sr, 1937-2015
Julia Denyse Seyl, 1937-2012
Daniel Peter Seyl, 1939-2025
Lawrence Anthony Seyl, 1947-2012

Walter Henry Seyl, 1910-1948 = Mary Catherine Schmidt, 1914-2005
Timothy F. Seyl, 1939-2013

Rowena Eleanor Seyl, 1917-1989 = Charles Roy McNeil, 1914-1972
Daniel Lawrence McNeil, 1943-2001
Jerald Thomas McNeil, 1946-

McNeil - my father's family

My grandparents, their children and their grandchildren

Daniel Charles McNeil, 1888-1966 = Emma Nettie Cote, 1883-1944

James Daniel McNeil, 1910-1976 = Eva Lange, 1913-2012
Robert James McNeil, 1937-
Linda Ann McNeil, 1941-2023
Kathleen Ruth McNeil, 1946-

Charles Roy McNeil, 1914-1972 = Rowena Eleanor Seyl, 1917-1989
Daniel Lawrence McNeil, 1943-2001
Jerald Thomas McNeil, 1946-

Ruth Nettie McNeil, 1919-1990 = Eldon Viers 1916-1981

Four Generations Family Tree Chart

This chart shows the birth and death dates for four generations in my family tree.

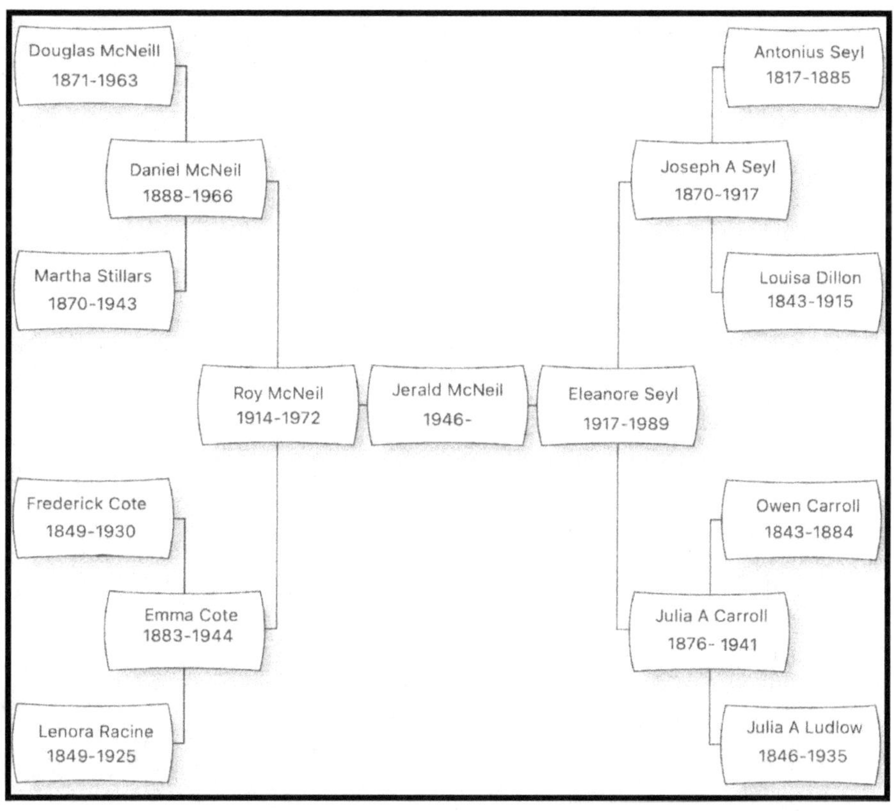

www.ingramcontent.com/pod-product-compliance
Lightning Source LLC
LaVergne TN
LVHW020709110826
845149LV00012B/2185

* 9 7 9 8 9 9 3 8 7 7 1 1 2 *